P9-EGD-002

J. WAGNER

KOREAN WAR

KOREAN WAR

STEPHEN BADSEY

GALLERY BOOKS
An imprint of W.H. Smith Publishers Inc.
112 Madison Avenue
New York, New York 10016

Published by Gallery Books
A Division of W H Smith Publishers Inc.
112 Madison Avenue
New York, New York 10016

Produced by
Brompton Books Corp.
15 Sherwood Place
Greenwich, CT 06830

ISBN 0-8317-6026-5
Printed in Hong Kong

PAGE 1: Specialist Fourth Class David K Brood of 5 RCT, US Army, rests from defending the Pusan perimeter.

PAGES 2-3: US Army M4A3 Shermans with their barrels elevated for indirect fire.

THESE PAGES: DUKW amphibious vehicles carry men of US 1st Marine Division toward the River Han after Inchon, September 1950.

CONTENTS

THE LEGACY OF HIROSHIMA

The Korean War began on 25 June 1950 with an attack by the forces of North Korea upon South Korea, a local war in a small Far Eastern country of which few Western people had even heard. By the time it ended on 27 July 1953, although all the fighting took place in Korea itself, it had involved, directly or indirectly, forces from nearly half the world, and brought a third world war closer than it had ever been. At the war's end, the United Nations Organization (UN) estimated the total casualties on all sides at nearly three million, including half a million dead. Other, unofficial, estimates put the number of Korean dead alone as high as four million. Yet for all its destructive power, the Korean conflict stands as history's first deliberately 'limited war,' the model on which peacekeeping in a dangerous world has been based ever since.

The causes of the Korean War go back to the very end of World War II, to 6 August 1945 when the first atomic bomb to be used in a war, dropped from a US Army Air Force B-29 Superfortress, exploded over the Japanese city of Hiroshima with the force of 16,000 tons of TNT, killing outright at least 80,000 of its 320,000 population. Josef Stalin, General Secretary of the Soviet Communist Party and dictator of the Soviet Union, already knew about the atomic bomb, both officially from US President Harry S Truman, and unofficially from the network of Soviet spies within the United States. At the time, the Soviet Union was at peace with Japan. Although there had been some fighting on the Soviet border with the Japanese puppet state of Manchukuo (modern Manchuria) in 1939, Stalin's government had signed a Pact of Friendship with the Japanese in April 1941. But, unknown to the Japanese, Stalin had also agreed with the Americans and British in 1943 that the Soviet Union would enter the war against Japan three

PAGES 6-7: The city of Hiroshima following the dropping of the American atomic bomb on 6 August 1945.

LEFT: Josef Stalin in his usual uniform as Generalissimo of the Soviet Union, 1949.

BELOW LEFT: Soviet troops during border clashes with the Japanese over Manchuria, May-June 1939.

RIGHT: US President Harry S Truman in 1946.

BELOW: Chairman Mao Tse-tung, taken shortly after the Korean War.

months after the defeat of Germany. In April 1945, as the war against Germany drew to a close, the Soviet Union withdrew from its Pact of Friendship and began to build up forces along the Manchukuo border.

As American and Soviet governments found themselves increasingly in conflict over the control of post-war Europe, particularly with regard to the new partitioned Germany, President Truman was anxious to exclude the Soviet Union from the occupation of Japan. Stalin was equally intent that Soviet forces should take part in the defeat of Japan. A rushed declaration of war was presented to the Japanese ambassador in Moscow on 8 August, and on the following day, as a second American atomic bomb devastated Nagasaki, Soviet armored columns crossed the Manchukuo border. The result was one of the most spectacular victories in modern military history with Soviet tanks overrunning the whole of Manchukuo – an area the size of Western Europe – in 15 days of *blitzkrieg*, completely routing the Japanese.

Linking up with the Soviets as they reached the southern border of Manchukuo was the Chinese Red Army under its charismatic leader Mao Tse-tung. As political head of the Chinese Communist Party, Mao had joined in a fragile United Front with the Chinese Nationalist government, or Kuomintang, under Generalissimo Chiang Kai-shek to resist Japanese aggression in 1937. Mao had come to believe that in China and the Far East it would be human determination and persistence in outlasting the enemy that would produce victory, not superior technology and firepower. His Red Army – renamed the People's Liberation Army (PLA) in 1946 – was almost entirely a force of peasant guerrilla fighters, with very few tanks, aircraft or artillery pieces, and his preferred strategy was one of protracted war to wear down the enemy. Once Japan was defeated, the Kuomintang government would be his next victim, and he looked to the Soviet Union for support.

Due to a quirk of history, the extreme far eastern border of the Soviet Union did not quite match the Manchukuo frontier. Along a 12-mile strip inland from the Sea of Japan, the border touched against the northern tip of Korea, and as Soviet tanks rolled into Manchukuo, Red Navy forces carried out a series of amphibious landings along the eastern Korean coast. On 15 August 1945 the Japanese surrendered, but the Soviets continued their advance, and by the 21st had taken the Korean port of Wonsan. Among those who followed the Soviet marines ashore at Wonsan was a 33-year-old Korean in the uniform of a Soviet Army major. His real name was Kim Sung Chu, but as a senior Korean communist he had taken the name of a dead guerrilla hero, Kim Il Sung. Within five years Kim Il Sung would once again attempt to unite his country by war.

Although the Japanese had surrendered to all the Allies, there were no American ground or naval forces within reach of Manchukuo to dispute the Soviet occupation, and the Americans were far more concerned with Soviet involvement in Japan than in Korea. On the night of 10 August officers of US Army Operations in Washington spent 30 minutes with a large-scale map to find a suitable partition line with the Soviets. No natural geographical feature crosses Korea, and since the Americans wanted the national capital of Seoul in their half of the country, they proposed the 38th Parallel. On

the 15th, as the Japanese surrender was announced, the Soviet Union accepted this offer, and its forces slowed down to reach their stop-line on 3 September. General Douglas MacArthur, the Supreme Commander Allied Powers (SCAP) for Japan and victor of the Southwest Pacific campaign, took the formal Japanese surrender in Tokyo Bay on the 2nd, but American forces did not land at Inchon, the port of Seoul, to administer South Korea until six days later.

Had Stalin wished, the Soviet Union could have occupied the whole Korean peninsula without opposition. The 38th Parallel was just one of many military stop-lines agreed between the Allies at the end of the war, and made no sense as any kind of permanent frontier. The Korean peninsula is about 600 miles long and 150 miles broad on average, giving a total area of 85,000 square miles. The Taebaek mountains, rising up to 9000 feet, run down the central and eastern part of the country, from which major rivers flow west or southwest. To the north the country is broken and mountainous, leading to the deep valley of the Yalu and Tumen rivers that mark the frontier with Manchuria. In 1945 the main line of communication was the railroad system running from Pusan in the southeast across to the west and up through Seoul and the main industrial center of Pyongyang toward the Yalu. Most of Korea's industry was concentrated north of the 38th Parallel, together with a population of about eight million, and the area formed part of the important Manchurian industrial region, centered on Mukden (modern Shenyang). South of the 38th Parallel the more fertile, open plains of Korea were home to a population of about 21 million and to most of the country's agriculture, the staple crop being rice.

The Korean coast has more than 3000 islands, of which the largest and most important is Cheju, roughly 70 miles southwest of the mainland. The Koreans are a

distinct racial group with a single language common to all peoples of the peninsula except for Cheju. By the end of World War II they had also spread throughout the Far East, with over 500,000 Koreans in Manchukuo and about 250,000 in Central Asia. Perhaps 150,000 members of the Korean Volunteer Corps fought with Mao's Chinese Red Army in World War II and many of these 'exiles' were destined to take part in the Korean War. Korea's chief religion was Buddhism but, as in many Far Eastern countries, a significant but influential minority was Christian. Korean communists professed atheism as a matter of course, and embarked on a policy of religious persecution in 1945.

From 1636 until modern times Korea survived as a puppet kingdom of the Chinese Empire. But with the rise of Japan and the eastward expansion of Russia in the nineteenth century, the country inevitably became a battleground. The southeast tip of Korea is less than 30 miles from the Japanese island of Tsushima and only 90 miles from the Japanese mainland, while the Korean capital of Seoul is less than 1000 miles from Tokyo, from Vladivostok, and from Peking. Following the Chinese defeat in the Sino-Japanese War of 1894-95, in which Japanese troops invaded Korea, they recognized Korean independence within the Japanese sphere of influence. Japanese dominance was confirmed by their victory in

FAR LEFT: Nagasaki after the American atomic bomb dropped on 9 August 1945, just as Soviet troops invaded Manchuria.

LEFT: Kim Il Sung, taken after he became leader of the People's Democratic Republic of Korea.

ABOVE: Japanese and Chinese warships in the Battle of the Yellow Sea, 1894, the key naval engagement of the Sino-Japanese War.

RIGHT: Japanese Imperial Guardsmen in Manchuria during the Russo-Japanese War of 1904-5.

War, later put it, 'we held the rather simplistic belief that all communist moves worldwide were dictated from Moscow and by Stalin personally.' Although many liberation movements looked to the Soviet Union for support, political life in countries emerging from World War II was often more complex than Washington understood, and Korea was no exception. A small Korean Communist Party was founded in Seoul in 1925 but was soon destroyed by the Japanese. Koreans in exile tended to join the Chinese Communist Party or even that of the Soviet Union, while others pursued independent courses. Not until 1939 did an indigenous Communist Group re-establish itself in Korea, chiefly in the south.

In September 1945, renamed the Korean Communist Party, this group proclaimed itself the government of the country, ruling through the People's Committees which it had established. South of the 38th Parallel the Americans simply ignored this attempt at government, and in the North it was overtaken by events as other communists returned to Korea in the wake of the Soviet Army and joined the People's Committees, ousting their predecessors. Among those who returned was Kim Il Sung, who had fled to the Soviet Union after the failure of the Manchukuo guerrilla campaign in 1941, but who

the Russo-Japanese War of 1904-5, in which Korea was the war's main theater. As a result of this war, Korea became a Japanese protectorate, and the Japanese deposed the last Korean emperor turning the country into a colony in 1910.

Finally, in 1942, the Japanese Home Ministry took control of Korea as an integral part of Japan. By this time there were over 750,000 Japanese living in Korea, and the country had been part of the Japanese Empire for two generations – longer than Arizona or Oklahoma had been part of the United States. When the Japanese took Manchuria from the Chinese to create Manchukuo in 1931, and when they turned against China itself in 1937, Koreans fought as soldiers in the Japanese Imperial Army, although always treated as second-class citizens. They were often used as guards for prisoner-of-war camps during World War II.

From the outset there was opposition to Japanese rule in Korea, and in 1919 there was a major rebellion in which over 70,000 Koreans died. Thereafter most dissidents moved overseas, some to start an ineffectual guerrilla campaign against the Japanese in Manchukuo after 1931. Naturally, China became a home for Koreans opposed to Japan and a Korean 'Provisional Government in Exile' was formed in Shanghai during World War I. In 1921 the exiles' president, Dr Syngman Rhee, gave up his post to become their Washington representative in the hope of gaining American support. Born in 1875, Dr Rhee was attractive to the Americans as a potential leader of postwar Korea: part of the country's intellectual elite, he was a convert to Christianity with an American education (his doctorate was from Princeton), he was violently opposed to Communism, and he had been imprisoned by the Japanese. Even so, because of its anti-communist stance Dr Rhee's Korean Democratic Party, formed in September 1945, was tainted in the eyes of many Koreans by some of its members' previous association with the Japanese.

'In those days,' as General Omar Bradley, Chairman of the Joint Chiefs of Staff (JCS) at the time of the Korean

LEFT: Dr Syngman Rhee as President of the Republic of Korea in 1950.

BELOW: C-47 Dakotas of the US Air Force being loaded with supplies to be flown in during the Berlin Airlift of 1948-49.

RIGHT: French troops fighting insurgents in the old French colony of Vietnam in 1951. Within three years the French would lose to the Viet Minh forces under Ho Chi Minh, which would take possession of North Vietnam.

was far from being a Soviet puppet.

President Franklin D Roosevelt, who had died in April 1945 leaving Vice-President Truman as his successor, had spoken often during World War II of a united world controlled by America, the Soviet Union, Britain and France as its 'four policemen' (sometimes adding Nationalist China as a fifth). In reality the war left Britain and France too weak to pursue their former role. In February 1947 the British Labour government under Clement Attlee announced that India, the keystone of the British Empire, was to be granted independence, and a month later informed the Americans that the British could no longer continue their traditional role in the Mediterranean and Middle East. In consequence, on 12 March 1947, President Truman announced to Congress his belief that 'it must be the policy of the United States to support free peoples who are resisting attempts of subjugation by armed minorities or by outside pressure.' This creed became known as the Truman Doctrine, an automatic commitment of American money, support and armed forces to any regime that was, or claimed to be, under threat or attack from communist aggression.

To American eyes, the events of the next few years were all part of a massive Soviet plot. The constant tension of the Cold War in Europe, the coming to power of a pro-Soviet communist government in Czechoslovakia in 1948, the communist 'Hellas' movement in Greece, Mao's Red Army in China, the Berlin Airlift in the winter of 1948-49 when Soviet forces closed the land routes to the city's Western sectors, the rise of the Viet Minh to oppose the French in Indochina, the start of the Communist Hukbalahap rebellion against American rule in the Philippines in 1946 and the Malayan Emergency against British rule in 1948 – all seemed from Washington to be part of a policy of world domination masterminded by Stalin, which America was obliged to resist.

Korea was both geographically and politically on the outer fringes of this policy of containment. As early as 1947 the JCS informed the president that Korea was

marginal to American security interests. The main American commitment was toward Europe, leading in 1949 to the US and Canada joining Western European nations in the North Atlantic Treaty Organization (NATO). Besides, although the Truman Doctrine implied a virtually open-ended global military commitment, America was at the same time dismantling the armed forces with which it had helped win World War II. The US Army, which had numbered 8,200,000 men in 1945 (including the Army Air Force) with over 90 fighting divisions, was cut back to barely 670,000 men and 10 skeleton divisions within five yars. The navy was similarly reduced from 64 capital ships and 3,300,000 men to 11 capital ships and 430,000 men, and the Marine Corps from 480,000 to 86,000 men. On 30 June 1949 the US withdrew its last troops from South Korea, leaving behind some 500 military advisors. To complete the process, on 12 January 1950 the Secretary of State, Dean Acheson, announced in a major speech an American 'defensive perimeter' in the Far East that, while including Japan and the Philippines, omitted Korea. Korea was strategically important enough to preserve for democracy, but not important enough to warrant a major war.

Before the onset of the Cold War, American armed forces could be reduced safely in peacetime because, with the continental United States virtually immune from invasion, one or two years could be given over to raising, equipping and training new armies in times of tension. Now, with America committed to overseas defense, this was no longer a realistic option. General Dwight D Eisenhower, the victor of Northwest Europe, warned on retirement as Army Chief of Staff in 1948 that 'on mobilization day of war with a major power we shall need a minimum force of 1,300,000 men' – about twice the number available.

Confident that it had the solution to this problem was the US Air Force, made independent of the army by the National Security Act of 1947. With 48 groups each of 30 bombers or 75 fighters it was better prepared for war than either the army or the navy. The air force view was that airpower and atomic weapons had made land warfare as fought in World War II virtually obsolete. The American monopoly of the atomic bomb – there was a stockpile of about 100 Nagasaki-type bombs by 1950 – was seen as a deterrent to any hostile action. If the deterrent failed then an atomic response would be the principal means of winning the war, supplemented by massive conventional air attacks. Even the Soviet Union's atomic bomb testing in 1949 failed to dent the air force's confidence.

In early 1950 the JCS presented to President Truman 'Plan Dropshot,' a planning exercise dealing with a hypothetical third world war between the United States and the Soviet Union. This document made grim reading, viewing the conflict as essentially a repeat of World War II but with atomic weapons. Europe would be the main theater, and American success would depend heavily on whether the United Kingdom could be kept as a base for its bombers. In the secondary Far East theater, South Korea was given barely half a sentence, the Americans expecting an enemy offensive to occupy the peninsula in a matter of days. The whole basis of American military thinking was that the next war would be against the Soviet Union, global in scale, and would depend on atomic bombs.

Meanwhile, against this global backdrop, the problems of a partitioned Korea increased as Soviet-American relations chilled into Cold War. An American-Soviet Joint Commission met in Seoul to resolve the problem of uniting Korea in March 1946, but abandoned the effort after two months. Violence in South Korea as left-wing and right-wing groups fought each other culminated in the massive left-wing 'autumn harvest' uprising throughout the country in October 1946. In an effort to provide some kind of order, the Americans instituted an Interim Legislative Assembly, and helped establish a formal South Korean Interim Government under Syngman Rhee, including many former Korean officials of the old Japanese Empire, in May 1947. In parallel with this, a Soviet-supervised election in the North in November 1946 returned an unsurprising 97 percent vote for the Korean National Democratic Front under Kim Il Sung, and led to the creation in February 1947 of a National People's Committee. The Joint Com-

mission met just once more, in May 1947, before the Americans passed the whole problem over to an international organization which they themselves had done the most to create, the United Nations.

On 14 November 1947 the UN General Assembly formally adopted an American proposal to establish a UN Temporary Commission on Korea (UNTCOK) to oversee unification. The Soviet Union, determined to see this fail, argued that since Soviet and American interests were involved the UN Security Council had first call on the matter, making UNTCOK an unconstitutional body, and none of its representatives were allowed into North Korea. As a result, elections were held only in the South under UNTCOK supervision in May 1948, returning Syngman Rhee as President of the Republic of Korea (ROK), which came officially into existence on 15 August. On the 25th Kim Il Sung held his own elections to which communist 'delegates' from the South were invited, and, victorious, formed the People's Democratic Republic of Korea (PDRK) which had its capital at Pyongyang. This was immediately recognized as the legitimate Korean government by the Soviet Union, which started to withdraw its own troops. Since Korea had not yet been unified, and since both the ROK and the PDRK each claimed to be the sole government of all Korea, the UN General Assembly resolved – despite Soviet protests – to continue UNTCOK on a long-term basis as the UN Commission on Korea (UNCOK), which returned to the South in February 1949.

In late 1948, to great American surprise, Mao Tse-tung embarked on a series of powerful offensives against the Chinese Nationalists, driving them out of mainland China to the small offshore island of Taiwan (Formosa)

LEFT: British troops on patrol during the Malayan Emergency of 1948-60, looking for communist insurgents.

BELOW: Troops of the Army of the Republic of Korea (ROKAs) on parade, 1949. Their weapons are American but their uniforms are still very Japanese in appearance.

in a matter of months. North Korean support was useful to Mao in Manchuria, where up to 20 percent of his forces were Koreans, including the majority of the 145,000-strong Fourth Field Army. On 1 October 1949 Mao proclaimed the creation of the People's Republic of China in Peking. Although the communist world, and even some non-aligned countries such as India, recognized Mao's China, the United States refused to do so, insisting that the Nationalists should keep the Chinese seat as a permanent member of the Security Council. In response, the Soviet Union withdrew from the Security Council on 13 January 1950, announcing that it would not return or recognize the legality of further Security Council resolutions until 'the representative of the Kuomintang group has been removed.' Six months later the Soviet delegates had still not returned, and American-Soviet relations remained at a very low ebb.

A particularly outspoken critic of the loss of China was General Douglas MacArthur, who as SCAP had become virtual ruler of Japan. MacArthur had hoped to secure the Republican Party nomination for the 1948 presidential election in opposition to Truman, and also played heavily in the complex politics of the Far East. As early as July 1947 he had informed Truman's officials that while Chiang Kai-shek's government 'might not be the best in the world they were on our side and should be supported,' and after the fall of China he continued to predict a possible communist attack upon Taiwan or South Korea, which he saw as part of the same problem. In August 1949 he announced publicly to President Rhee that he would defend South Korea 'as I would California,' and – even more ominously – that 'nothing shall prevent the ultimate unity of your people as free men of a free nation.' That such pronouncements were out of step with American government policy mattered little to MacArthur, who regarded himself (with some justification) as a more important figure in the Far East than Truman.

Political dealings between the American government and communist countries were not helped by the start of the notorious 'McCarthy Era' of American politics in early 1950, in which the junior senator from Wisconsin, Joseph McCarthy, was able to establish Congressional committees to investigate his own wild claims concerning major communist infiltration of the American government. For the next four years, McCarthy ran a witch-hunt in Washington and throughout America in search of a virtually non-existent communist menace. The Truman administration, and its conduct of the Korean War, were to function against a background of political hatred such as the United States has seldom seen in its history.

Meanwhile, Syngman Rhee's government in South Korea appeared increasingly unstable. In May 1948 there was a serious uprising on Cheju island, followed by another in the major southeastern port of Yosu in October, leading to a sustained Maoist-style guerrilla campaign by about 6000 opponents of the South Korean government for the next two years, and making the work of UNCOK virtually impossible. Not very surprisingly, President Rhee blamed North Korea, which provided training and encouragement, but few actual weapons, for the guerrillas.

Matters became worse on 4 May 1949 at Kaesong on the 38th Parallel when troops on both sides opened fire in the first of nearly 100 serious 'incidents,' skirmishes which dragged on for days across the disputed border. Syngman Rhee, in aggressive mood, pleaded with the United States to allow him the armed forces and military hardware to attack North Korea. Understandably, the Americans were in no hurry to do so. Instead, the South Korean government struck back against the guerrillas using officers who had served with the Japanese, and by early summer 1950, despite all its problems, the South was winning the guerrilla war.

On 19 June, with the guerrillas defeated, the North Korean government launched a new initiative calling for the 'peaceful unification' of Korea through elections, which was interpreted in the South and by the United States as just one more political maneuver. The course of action predicted by most Intelligence analysts was for Kim Il Sung to renew his support for the guerrillas and continue his political pressure. Instead, from early June, North Korean forces began to move into position preparatory to a lightning strike across the 38th Parallel.

The Korean People's Army (*Cho-son In-Min Kun*), or KPA, was formally established on 8 February 1948 with troops from Mao's Korean Volunteer Corps, retrained by its Soviet advisors to reflect their own military doctrines. Most communist armies in the Far East were mass peasant guerrilla forces on the Maoist model, but the KPA was trained to overwhelm an enemy in days. By June 1950 its best troops were back from service with

BELOW: Senator Joseph McCarthy during a hearing of the Committee on Un-American Activities.

the Chinese PLA, and it had been reorganized into 10 infantry divisions, each having three regiments of three infantry battalions, an artillery regiment of three 12-gun 122mm battalions, and an assault gun battalion of 12 Soviet-made SU-76s. The divisions were numbered from one to seven (the 3rd Division being the Guards Division), and 10, 13 and 15, the last three being formed between March and June 1950. Smaller and more lightly equipped than its Western counterpart, a KPA division totaled 12,092 men at full strength.

The KPA's sole tank unit was the 105th Armored Brigade, upgraded to 105 Armored Division shortly after the start of the war and equipped with 120 aging Soviet T34/85 tanks. Equipment and weapons came almost entirely from the Soviet Union; most of World War II vintage. For a conventional 'blitzkrieg' army the KPA was badly lacking in motorized forces, in firepower and in the other crucial element of lightning war – airpower. Its air component was a single fighter regiment of about 70 Soviet-made Yak-3s, Yak-7s, Yak-9s and LA-7s, and a ground-attack regiment of 60 I1-10s, all piston-engined aircraft from World War II. The naval forces consisted of torpedo boats, which for a peninsula like Korea was to have important consequences, plus about a division of marines. In total, the KPA numbered roughly 223,000 men. Although the Soviet Union rushed new weapons and equipment to North Korea after the start of the war, there is little evidence to support the American claim that they did so before the war started, or that a Soviet general drew up the KPA attack plan.

The Army of the Republic of Korea (*Tae-Han Min-Guk Yuk-Kun*), or ROKA (its soldiers were known as 'ROKs' to the Americans), was an armed police, elevated to the status of an army on the founding of the Republic of Korea on 15 August 1948, and was not comparable to the KPA in fighting value. By June 1950 it had seven weak infantry divisions, numbered from one to three and five to eight (the number four being unlucky to Koreans), plus a Capital Security Command, renamed the Capitol Division after the war started. The Korean Marine Corps (KMC), founded in April 1949 on the model of the US Marines, consisted only of 1 Regiment (three battalions) and the independent 5th Battalion. On paper each ROKA division, ilke those of the KPA, should have had three regiments of three battalions each, plus an artillery battalion and a tank company. In fact the ROKA had no tanks, only 27 M8 armored cars in its 1st Cavalry Regiment, and just three 105mm artillery battalions, supporting 7th Division, 8th Division, and 17th Regiment (part of the Capitol Division). Of the ROKA divisions, only 1st Division, 6th Division, 7th Division and the Capitol Division were at full strength, but were still far weaker than a Western division at 10,948 men of all ranks. The ROKs had no heavy mortars, no mines, no medium artillery, no aircraft and virtually no navy, and morale in the understrength divisions was low. In total the force numbered roughly 98,000 men, about half of them occupied with the guerrilla war in South Korea, and the remainder with policing the 38th Parallel. This was the armed might with which Syngman Rhee persistently threatened to attack North Korea.

The other major factor in the North Korean calculations was the United States. The distance from the 38th Parallel to the southernmost tip of the Korean mainland is little more than 200 miles. Could Kim Il Sung's troops defeat the ROKA and occupy the whole peninsula before American forces could intervene? The nearest American fighting units were in Japan, part of MacArthur's multiple command as SCAP, Commander-in-Chief Far East (CINCFE) and Commanding General US Army Far East. The Far Eastern Air Forces (FEAF) under Lieutenant-General George E Stratemeyer included the USAF Fifth Air Force (Major-General Earle E 'Pat' Partridge). It was based in Japan and comprised three wings (about 100 aircraft) of F-80C Shooting Star jet fighters, a reconnaissance squadron of RF-80s, and two all-weather fighter squadrons flying the piston-engined F-86 Twin Mustang, plus a bombardment wing of B-26 Invader medium bombers and a transport wing of C-54 Skymasters. These were enough to drive the KPA aircraft from the skies, but probably not enough to stop its ground forces. More worrying for the KPA was the wing of B-29 Superfortresses of the Twentieth Air Force based on Guam, which could carry atomic bombs. The Commander-in-Chief Pacific (CINCPAC), Admiral Arthur Radford, had available the Seventh Fleet under Vice-Admiral Arthur D Struble, but this would not be able to reach Korea for days. For a time US ground forces would have to rely on air support alone.

American ground forces in Japan consisted of the 7th, 24th, 25th and 1st Cavalry Divisions (which despite its name was an infantry formation) which were grouped as the Eighth Army under Lieutenant-General Walton H 'Bulldog' Walker. The full strength of an American division was 18,900 men when mobilized and 12,500 in peacetime. In June 1950, the 25th Division mustered 13,000 men, but the other divisions were each over 1000 men short even of their peacetime strength. All except one of the infantry regiments were down to two understrength battalions each, none of the regiments had tank companies, the divisional tank companies were equipped only with light tanks, and artillery units were at two-thirds strength in both men and guns. There was even a serious shortage of ammunition. The Eighth Army's readiness to fight outside Japan was very low. Finally, there were several political questions: would the Americans fight for South Korea, how quickly could they respond, and what weapons would they use? While Truman and his advisors were making up their minds over the strategy to adopt, the war might easily end in a North Korean victory.

On 25 June 1950 the only Soviet troops in North Korea were a few hundred 'advisers,' and the precise Soviet role in the start of the war has never been clear. Was the Korean War, as it seemed to the Americans in 1950, part of a master plan engineered by Stalin? Kim Il Sung is known to have visited Moscow just once before the war, in February 1949, and from a distance the North Korean attack looks less like part of some complex Soviet global strategy and more like a local gamble by Kim Il Sung to unite his country. The most that can be said is that Stalin probably knew about the plan beforehand, without necessarily approving of it. But, just as throughout its history Korea had been dominated by greater empires, so in 1950 other powers had large parts to play in the Korean War. Above all, it could never be forgotten that this was the first war of the era of atomic weapons. The mushroom cloud of Hiroshima, as much as the dead hand of history, hung over the Korean War from its beginning to its end.

GENERAL MACARTHUR'S WAR

About 40 miles north of Seoul, the arbitrary frontier of the 38th Parallel cuts off the southern portion of the Onjin peninsula from the rest of South Korea, making it difficult to hold and impossible for the ROKA to defend. In the early hours of 25 June, after a week of border incidents and provoked by heavy KPA shelling, the ROKA's 17th Regiment responded by attacking and briefly capturing the town of Haeju. Ever since, the North Koreans have claimed that they had done no more than defend themselves against a South Korean invasion attempt. There is, however, no doubt that the KPA invasion of South Korea was both pre-planned and unexpected. Apart from the 17th Regiment (of the Capitol Division) only four ROKA divisions held the 38th Parallel: the 1st and 7th Divisions covering Seoul, the 6th Division in the center of the country and the 8th Division on the east coast across the Taebaek mountains, in total 40,000 men. The ROKA commander was Major-General Chae Pyongdok, and the commander along the 38th Parallel was Major-General Kim Sok-Won, who like many of his officers had fought in the Japanese Imperial Army, and who had been decorated for bravery by Emperor Hirohito.

With Kim Il Sung as Supreme Commander, the KPA was commanded by General Choi Yung Kun, who formed his seven veteran divisions, together with 105th Armored Brigade, into a Soviet-style 'Front' under General Kim Chaek. Starting at 0400 hours local time, the attack plan was like a miniature of the great Soviet offensives of World War II. The Taebaek mountains split the Front naturally into two armies, of which the First Army in the west made the main thrust: the 6th Division overran the Onjin peninsula, while the 105th Armored Brigade led the 1st, 3rd and 4th Divisions down the Uijongbu corridor, the historic invasion route toward Seoul. Meanwhile the Second Army's 2nd and 7th Divisions tied down the ROKA's strong 6th Division, and on the east coast the 5th Division took on the ROKA's 8th Division, aided by a KPA Marine landing behind the

ROKA position. The KPA generals judged that they had supplies and men for a two-month war, time enough to wipe out the ROKA and occupy Korea before the Americans could intervene.

In the face of this surprise attack by about 95,000 troops the under-equipped ROKA formations, without antitank weapons to oppose the T34/85s and SU-76s, simply disintegrated. The 17th Regiment abandoned the Onjin peninsula by sea, leaving its precious artillery behind, while the 8th Division fell back in headlong flight. In four days' fighting the KPA First Army advanced to occupy Seoul, from where President Rhee's government fled to Taejon. Supply problems then forced the Front to pause for two days. The UNCOK observers, before being evacuated to safety in Japan on 27 June, reported to the United Nations that the North Korean attack had been a deliberate and unprovoked act of aggression. Under the circumstances, there was little else that they could have said.

0400 on Sunday, 25 June, in Korea was 1400 hours on Saturday, 24 June, in Washington. But it was not until around midnight in Washington that it became clear that this was an invasion and not another border incident. What made this war unusual was that President Truman chose to act through the medium of the United Nations. Founded on 26 June 1945 in San Francisco, the UN was intended to be an organization to prevent wars, not to fight them, and its members not only gave up the right to wage war except in self-defense or by UN order, but also imposed the same restrictions on the rest of the world. (All but 23 of the then 74 sovereign states in existence joined the UN in 1945, the remainder being chiefly neutrals or Axis states of World War II with their empires – neither Korea was a member.) The teeth of the United Nations was the Security Council, meeting in 1950 at its temporary headquarters at Lake Success rather than in New York City. This consisted of five permanent members – the 'Big Five' of America, the Soviet Union, Britain, France and China – plus six temporary

PREVIOUS PAGES: Two F-9F Panther jet fighters of the US Marines on the deck of the aircraft carrier USS *Leyte Gulf* off the coast of Korea, July 1950.

LEFT: Members of UNCOK at a press conference in Japan on 28 June following their successful evacuation from South Korea.

members. The votes of all five permanent members, plus at least one other, were required to pass a Security Council Resolution. In theory a Military Staff Committee should have controlled standing UN military forces, but this had proved impractical and instead the UN depended on voluntary troop contributions from all its members.

At 1800 hours local time on Sunday the 25th, after less than four hours debate, the Security Council voted nine-to-nil, with Yugoslavia abstaining and the Soviet Union recorded absent, to adopt the American-sponsored Resolution S/1501 which called for North Korean forces to withdraw to the 38th Parallel and for member nations 'to render every assistance to the United Nations in the execution of this resolution and to refrain from giving assistance to the North Koreans.' If the Soviet Union had known beforehand of the precise North Korean plan, and had wished to delay or prevent UN action, then their delegate should have been present to veto this key resolution.

What is harder to understand is that they continued to stay away. On 27 June the Security Council passed S/1511, which noted the lack of North Korean response to S/1501 and asked 'that the members of the United Nations furnish such assistance to the Republic of Korea as may be necessary to repel an armed attack,' and on 7 July it adopted the Anglo-French Resolution S/1588 authorizing a unified United Nations Command to conduct the war under an American commander. Only on 1 August did the Soviet delegation return to the Security Council, assuming the presidency by monthly rotation. By this time 15 other countries had agreed to join America in sending troops to South Korea, and a further five to send medical aid. Although the total UN contribution was small compared to those of the United States and the ROKA, never exceeding 44,000 troops, this demonstration of international solidarity was politically invaluable to the Americans.

It may never be known what the Soviet Union was trying to achieve in its handling of the Korean crisis. In Washington, however, the suspicion grew rapidly that Korea was nothing less than a Soviet feint attack on a global scale, designed to suck in American troops and resources, and so leave Western Europe dangerously unprotected. As General Bradley observed, Korea was 'the wrong war, in the wrong place, at the wrong time, with the wrong enemy.' These suspicions joined with fear of global atomic war and with the desire to make the UN work as a force for world peace. American strategy was to restore South Korea, not to occupy the North, and to avoid an aggressive policy which might bring Communist China or even the Soviet Union into the war. An immediate offer by Chiang Kai-shek of three Nationalist Chinese divisions to serve in Korea with the UN forces was, after brief consideration, turned down by Truman as too provocative.

Impressive though the American and UN response was at the level of global politics, it was at first worth very little in South Korea, where the immediate problem was to stop the KPA advance. On the night of 26 June Truman in Washington authorized MacArthur as CINCFE to help the ROKA with American air and sea power, but only south of the 38th Parallel. Even before this decision, American F-82s out of Japan, flying cover for transport aircraft over Seoul, had clashed with KPA fighters,

shooting one down. On the 29th, as MacArthur made a personal flight of inspection to Korea, Truman instructed him to deploy American ground troops in small numbers to support the ROKA. MacArthur's response was that two American divisions were needed at once if Korea was to be saved. Even before his flight, MacArthur had violated his orders by instructing General Stratemeyer to bomb targets above the 38th Parallel, a decision not confirmed in Washington until a National Security Council meeting that evening. On 10 July Truman confirmed MacArthur as Commander-in-Chief United Nations Command (CINCUNC) for Korea.

It was MacArthur's behavior in these crucial days which guaranteed a major American commitment to defend South Korea. In 1950 General of the Army Douglas MacArthur was fit, alert, energetic and 70 years old, at the end of an astonishing military career. Himself the son of a lieutenant-general, MacArthur had never known any other life but the army, and any other standard for himself but excellence. He had graduated top of his class from West Point in 1903, reached the rank of brigadier-general in World War I as one of the most decorated officers in the army, and had been the youngest ever Superintendent of West Point. From 1930 to 1935 he had served as Army Chief of Staff, and in World War II had become one of only three Americans to command an active Theater of Operations.

Yet despite his achievements, there was always a question mark over MacArthur. By nature he was autocratic and flamboyant, fond of bold declamations and showy military operations. General Eisenhower, who served on his staff in the 1930s, joked that he had studied amateur dramatics under MacArthur for five years. His unsuccessful defense of the Philippines against the Japanese in 1942 became best known for the catch-phrase 'I shall return,' and for his rather doubtful winning of the Medal of Honor as commanding general. As a theater commander he proved uninterested in inter-Allied and inter-service cooperation, conducting private wars of intrigue with the navy and refusing to allow British or Australian officers on his staff. As SCAP in Japan, after five years as virtual dictator of the country, his staff and circle of friends closely resembled some strange American version of an oriental court, and failed completely to predict the North Korean attack on South Korea. But to Americans who shared his own fiercely Republican politics MacArthur, ready throughout his career to answer back even to presidents, remained a war hero and military genius.

MacArthur's views on war were those of the World War I generals under whose influence his own career had progressed. Like many of the same generation, he fully accepted the right of a country's political leaders to declare war, but saw war as a moral evil to be engaged in when all political solutions had failed. If war was the breakdown of politics, then the best strategy was to end the war as quickly as possible through military victory, and the best judges of how to do this were the country's professional military leaders. After victory had been secured, political leaders could once again assume their dominant place; in war their only function was to support their military commanders, or to replace them. To MacArthur 'victory' meant the total destruction of North Korea, and of any other power which chose to assist North Korea, and any political attempt to interfere in

LEFT: A US Army 105mm howitzer of the 24th Division in action in support of ROKA forces, 15 July 1950. Artillery firepower was to be crucial in holding the KPA advance.

RIGHT: M-26 Pershing tanks holding the line of the Naktong River, 15 August 1950.

BELOW: A KPA supply column destroyed on the road just south of Konju, South Korea, by US Air Force F-80 Shooting Stars operating from Japan, 17 July 1950.

this would result only in a longer war, increased bloodshed, and ultimate defeat. MacArthur's view of political and military relations in the Korean War became clear when, on 31 July, with the situation in South Korea still critical, he flew to Taiwan to confer with Chiang Kai-shek, who announced to the press next day that he looked forward to serving once again with his 'old comrade in arms, General MacArthur.' A harassed Truman at once dispatched an envoy to Japan to explain American government policy to MacArthur. It was the first of many such incidents in the war.

The initial ground contingent from the US Eighth Army, Task Force Smith (1/2 1st Infantry Regiment and 52nd Field Artillery Battalion) from the 24th Division landed in South Korea on 1 July, and next day pushed up to Osan, 10 miles south of Seoul. It was just in time to join in a second ROKA rout. In the four days of fighting from 30 June, the KPA Front broke through the ROKA positions north of the River Han, and on 5 July Task Force Smith, which like the rest of the US Army was under strength, under trained, under equipped and far too small for its mission, was swept away by the KPA's 4th Division and the 105th Armored Division, losing half its men and all its heavy equipment in 24 hours. The survivors fell back on the rest of the 24th Division, which conducted a fighting withdrawal back to the River Kum just north of Taejon, from where the ROKA government fled to Taegu.

The situation was so serious that on 9 July MacArthur appears to have asked for atomic bombs to be used. But

despite the addition of the 12th, 13th and 15th Divisions the KPA advance was being slowed, taking seven days to cover the 40 miles to the Kum. On the 13th Lieutenant-General Walker set up his headquarters as the Eighth US Army in Korea (EUSAK) and next day President Rhee took the desperate measure of placing all ROKA forces directly under Walker's command. From this date, Walker directed the ROKA forces through their Chief-of-Staff, Lieutenant-General Chung Il Kwon.

The battle for the River Kum and Taejon began on 14 July, and the US 24th Division discovered what was to be a major problem throughout the war: the unreliability of ROKA forces in defense. While the KPA's 3rd and 4th Divisions simply walked past the 24th Division's flanks, the KPA's 6th Division to the west, mopping up the remains of the ROKA's 7th Division, drove virtually unopposed all the way to the south coast at Mokpo and Yosu. By July 20 the 24th Division had been driven out of Taejon, badly mauled and with its commanding general missing (he was taken prisoner and later awarded the Medal of Honor for his defense).

Despite this, MacArthur advised Truman on 19 July that the two weeks bought by the 24th Division had cost the KPA its chance of victory. The US 25th Division and 1st Cavalry Division were already arriving in Korea, while the 29th Regiment, 5th Regimental Combat Team (RCT) and the 2nd Division would all reach Korea from the USA before the end of the month, together with six battalions of M26 Pershing and M4 Sherman tanks and the British 27th Infantry Brigade. Meanwhile a last defensive line was being formed in what became known as the 'Pusan perimeter,' running from Yongdok on the east coast across to the valley of the Naktong River and south to Koje island.

On reaching the perimeter line on 24 July the ROKA was reorganized, taking over the northern sector from Yongdok to Hamchang. The unreliable 2nd, 5th and 7th Divisions were disbanded, the 8th and Capitol Divisions were formed into ROKA I Corps, the 1st and 6th Divisions into ROKA II Corps, and the 3rd Division kept as a reserve. Meanwhile, the exceptional KPA 6th Division, which had pushed along the coast almost to Masan, 50 miles from Pusan itself, was just stopped by regiments of the US 24th Division and the newly arrived 25th Division. With the 1st Cavalry Division and the rest of the 25th Division in the center Walker had 47,000 American troops and 45,000 ROKs, facing perhaps 70,000 KPA troops.

In the areas which they had overrun, the North Koreans re-instated the People's Committees, and made good the losses of the KPA by conscripting locals of military age on the grounds that they were citizens of the unified People's Democratic Republic of Korea. These new conscripts were hardly the equals of the old KPA veterans of Mao's forces. Faced with the prospect of being conscripted by either side, many Koreans of military age joined the elderly, women and children as refugees. Meanwhile the guerrilla war in South Korea came back to life, even inside the Pusan perimeter, where the ROKs and Americans took drastic reprisal actions. Up to the end of August over 67,000 suspected guerrillas had been killed by ROKs and American troops, and about the same number captured or surrendered, to be sent to squalid prison camps. Treatment of prisoners on both sides in the Korean War was frequently barbaric. After the battle at Taejon KPA forces executed between 5000 and 7000 politically suspect civilians. The most that can be said for the ROKA is that its treatment of its enemies was rarely as brutal or as systematic.

In World War II, the United States had relied heavily on armor, artillery and air strikes to offset the sometimes poor quality of its infantry. In Korea the situation was even worse, with ground troops being dispatched to the fighting zone after a minimum of basic training. One bad case, the 29th Regiment which reached Korea on 24 July, contained 400 raw recruits who had joined the

RIGHT: A US Army 105mm howitzer in action on the Pusan perimeter, 4 August 1950.

BELOW LEFT: British troops of the 27th Infantry Brigade about to set out on patrol shortly after their arrival in Korea.

BELOW: Frontline treatment of American casualties in Korea.

LEFT: The oil refinery at the North Korean port of Wonsan being bombed by aircraft from the US Seventh Fleet, July 1950.

BELOW: The ruins of the Chinnampo Ore Smelting Plant, the largest in North Korea, following a raid by US Air Force B-29 Superfortresses in August 1950.

RIGHT: A US Air Force F-51 Mustang of 18th Fighter-Bomber Wing at the moment of release of its two napalm bombs over North Korea, August 1950.

BELOW RIGHT: The town of Chinju in South Korea under attack by the US Fifth Air Force in an effort to stop the KPA drive on Pusan, August 1950.

regiment four days previously. But by 1 August, as Lieutenant-General Walker ordered all forces to retreat to the perimeter behind the Naktong, total American air superiority had been established over North and South Korea. On Okinawa the 3rd Bombardment Wing of B-29s had been joined by the 19th Bombardment Wing — each aircraft carrying a 20,000 pound bomb-load. Within the perimeter itself Taegu airfield was still open and a Fifth Air Force/Joint Army Operations Center was functioning by 24 July. Close-support strikes came from a wing of F-51 Mustangs, including 77 Squadron, Royal Australian Air Force. Two aircraft carriers from the US Seventh Fleet, flying jet and piston-engined strike aircraft, had also arrived off the east coast of Korea, together with four smaller Royal Navy carriers. Together they dominated the seas, making any KPA attempt to outflank the perimeter by amphibious landing or resupply by sea impossible, as well as adding to Walker's firepower over the battlefield.

Not surprisingly, the US Air Force had its own master plan on how to win the war, and it had little to do with the ground battle. Strategic Air Command (SAC) sought permission at this time simply to bomb flat the five largest cities in North Korea in the belief that this would force Kim Il Sung to seek peace. The idea was rejected in Washington as barbaric as well as contrary to American war aims. The theory that air power alone could win a war would not, after all, be tried out in Korea. Yet, as they themselves pointed out, over the next three years the Fifth Air Force and SAC caused far more damage, and killed far more civilians in North and South Korea, than their original plan would have cost.

The battle to hold the Pusan perimeter depended on a United States Army that, for one of the few times in its history, was badly trained and equipped, coupled with a ROK Army of frightening unpredictability, together holding off the attacks of a rapidly weakening North Korean Army. The whole battle was dominated by the weight of artillery fire, napalm and high-explosive bombs that Lieutenant-General Walker could bring to bear on the communist attacks. The lack of good quality infantry was so great that on 2 August the US 1st Provisional Marine Brigade, which MacArthur had hoped to use for an amphibious landing elsewhere, was deployed to the perimeter. Here it joined in a limited offensive with US 25th Division and 5th RCT on 7 August to push the enemy back from Chinju. This had to be quickly called off when the KPA 4th Division, which had begun to infiltrate across the Naktong on the 5th, threatened Yonsan in the US 24th Division's sector.

The Marines were promptly re-attached to the 24th Division for a counterattack, and by 18 August the KPA had been driven back to its start lines. This, the 'First Battle of the Naktong Bulge,' was regarded by the Marines as one of the hardest fights in their history. At the same time, the KPA 105th Armored Division led the bulk of the First Army (6th, 7th, 9th and 10th Divisions) in a strike at the northwest corner of the perimeter, on a line between the US 1st Cavalry Division and the ROKA 1st Division, which brought Taegu under artillery fire by 18 August, causing the ROK government to make its final retreat to Pusan. Reinforcing the ROKA 1st Division

with a RCT from the US 25th Division, Walker again counterattacked in the 'Battle of the Bowling Alley,' a valley north of Taegu, which began on the 18th and ended six days later – once again the KPA failed to break through.

A last attempt by the KPA 5th Division to turn the eastern flank of the perimeter along the coast actually cut off the ROKA's 3rd Division at Tokong-ni, but the advantages of seapower showed as the division was taken off by sea and redeployed, together with the Capitol Division, to halt the KPA drive at Pohang-dong on 20 August. As long as a defensive line could be held, there was no way through the firepower that Walker could deploy to support it.

By the end of August, Walker had some 83,000 American combat troops in position and had taken over 10,000 casualties. Size and losses of the ROKA had very little meaning, given the basic unreliability of its soldiers, many of whom had been redeployed to lines-of-communication duties to guard against guerrillas. To improve the situation MacArthur instituted the 'Katusa' (Korean Augmentation To US Army) scheme, whereby 22,000 selected ROKA soldiers were to be trained in Japan before being sent to American combat units, as many as 100 to a company on a 'buddy' system. It was hoped that the Katusas would increase the numbers in American units, improve South Korean fighting quality and American confidence in it, and help overcome the notorious unthinking racism of the average American recruit.

BELOW LEFT: A private of 27 RCT 'The Wolfhounds,' US 25th Division, firing a .30-caliber Browning medium machine-gun during the 'Battle of the Bowling Alley,' near Taegu, 20 August 1950.

RIGHT: American casualties being evacuated by air from Pusan airfield to Japan, August 1950.

BELOW: Members of the US 25th Division display a captured North Korean flag following the major KPA offensive of 5 August to take the Pusan perimeter.

US armed forces had been racially segregated until 1948, with blacks kept out of combat units, and the American slang insult for an oriental, a 'Gook,' actually derived from *Guk*, the Korean word for themselves. Veterans recalled that in Korea American soldiers would check the sights on their rifles by sniping at the peasants working the rice fields as if they were paper targets. All this could be overcome with time and training, but the Katusa scheme, although officially pronounced a success, was abandoned by the end of the year because of 'language difficulties.'

The final attempt of the KPA to breach the Pusan perimeter began with a general offensive on the night of 31 August. In the South, the KPA's 6th and 7th Divisions broke through the US 25th Division's positions, threatening Masan again. In the Naktong Bulge the US 2nd Division, which had replaced the 24th Division, was split almost in two by infiltration from the KPA's 2nd, 4th, 9th and 10th Divisions, while the US 1st Cavalry Division, defending Taegu, was pushed back by a combined onslaught from the 1st, 3rd and 13th Divisions. Farther east, the 8th and 15th Divisions drove the ROKA

LEFT: A North Korean T-34/85 tank abandoned after the bridge which it was crossing was hit by American fire.

BELOW: American heavy mortars in action from a carefully sandbagged position.

RIGHT: American troops resting and cleaning their weapons.

BELOW RIGHT: A US Army 105mm howitzer of the 52nd Field Artillery, part of the original Task Force Smith, in action.

II Corps (1st, 6th and 8th Divisions) back from Yong-chon, while the 5th and 12th Divisions threatened to un-hinge the whole UN position by driving the ROKA I Corps (Capitol and 3rd Divisions) away from the coast. By 5 September the situation was critical, and Lieutenant-General Walker briefly considered a fall-back to a final defensive line within the perimeter. But over the next three days American firepower, and Walker's own aggressive personal leadership, began to tell, and by the 8th the KPA was once again being driven back all along the perimeter. Walker declared that 'if it had not been for the air support that we received from the Fifth Air Force, we should not have been able to stay in Korea.'

Because of MacArthur's rapid response at the start of the war, the KPA had lost its gamble. It was not only defeated but exhausted, at the very end of its supply lines, all of which stretched back along the main railroad through the occupied South Korean capital of Seoul. Now, from his headquarters in Japan, MacArthur began to mount an operation which once again demonstrated his own extraordinary military genius, an amphibious landing far behind the KPA lines at Inchon, the port of Seoul. MacArthur had first conceived of the Inchon landing on visiting South Korea on 29 June, the fourth day of the war, and since then, while reports of nothing but disaster reached SCAP headquarters, his staff had worked to make it a reality. It was an operation which would end the existing Korean War within two months, only to start another war, far more destructive and deadly, which would in the end destroy MacArthur himself.

LEFT: British troops of the recently arrived 29th Infantry Brigade greet American soldiers on the Naktong River, September 1950.

RIGHT: US Army 'Long Tom' 155mm heavy artillery pieces of the 25th Infantry Division in action on the Pusan perimeter.

BELOW RIGHT: An 8-inch howitzer of the US artillery, also in action on the Pusan perimeter.

BELOW LEFT: British troops of 1/Middlesex Regiment, 27th Infantry Brigade, hitching a ride toward the front in an American 6x6 truck.

BELOW: US artillerymen at their plotting table with a 105mm howitzer in the background, September 1950.

ALL THE
WAY BACK

'We drew up a list of every conceivable and natural handicap,' remembered Lieutenant-Commander Arlie Capps, one of the US Seventh Fleet's experts on amphibious landings, 'and Inchon had 'em all.' The tidal range inside Inchon harbor was 32 feet, leaving about five miles of exposed mudflats at low tide, and the fierce current of the Flying Fish Channel, the only approach; to the harbor at high tide. Only on two suitable dates, 15 September and 11 October, did spring tides provide enough water for the crucial LSTs (Landing Ship, Tank) to get ashore, and these came in the middle of the typhoon season. Guarding Inchon harbor was the island of Wolmi-do, which would have to be secured in the morning of the attack while the main landing force sat out at sea to wait for the evening tide, forfeiting any chance of surprise or of making a major advance before nightfall.

The landing itself would be not onto beaches but over the Inchon harbor wall, needing scaling ladders. Inchon lay on an easily defended peninsula, and only a few miles inland was the natural defensive barrier of the River Han which covered Seoul itself. Apart from this, the two divisions needed to make the landing were not available, and there were not enough LSTs in the Seventh Fleet to put them ashore. As Rear-Admiral James H Doyle, the fleet's Amphibious Group Commander, put it to the final planning conference in Tokyo on 23 August, 'the best I can say is that Inchon is not impossible.'

What swung this conference, which included senior JCS representatives, in favor of Inchon was a highly impassioned speech by MacArthur, who argued that all the factors working against the landing would contribute to its surprise and success. The KPA position at Pusan had become so fragile that a successful landing deep across its only practical supply line would cause it to shatter. MacArthur gambled that Inchon would be lightly defended, and that if he could get troops ashore everything else would follow. There was little chance of complete surprise, but following US Army doctrine it was only essential for the enemy to be caught unprepared and unable to respond fast enough to make a difference. Thanks to MacArthur the landing, codenamed Operation Chromite, was approved.

The first problem was assembling the troops. Plans to use the 1st Provisional Marine Brigade (based on the 5th Marines) and the 1st Cavalry Division were abandoned early on when they were needed at Pusan. On 10 July, MacArthur and Lieutenant-General Lemuel C Sheppard, Commander Fleet Marine Force Pacific, asked the JCS to increase the 1st Provisional Marine Brigade by two further regiments to form the 1st Marine Division for the operation. With the assumption that airpower and atomic weapons had made amphibious landings obsolete, the strength and fortunes of the US Marines, like the army, were at a low ebb. Of the two additional regiments, the 1st Marines was a mixture of serving Marines and reservists recalled at two weeks' notice, while the 7th Marines was scraped together from detachments all over the world. Lieutenant-General Walker at first refused to release the 5th Marines from the Pusan perimeter until finally over-ruled by a direct order from MacArthur. The second division detailed for Chromite, the 7th Division, was the last Eighth Army division still in Japan and had been cannibalized to bring the other divisions up to strength. Despite a hurried addition of ROKA

PREVIOUS PAGES: Amphibious tractors (Amtracs) of the US 1st Marine Division making a landing at Wonsan, 26 October 1950.

LEFT: American and British warships carrying out the preliminary bombardment of Inchon and Wolmi-do, 13 September 1950.

ABOVE RIGHT: Amtracs of the 1st Marine Division heading for the landing at Inchon, 15 September 1950.

RIGHT: General Douglas MacArthur watches the Inchon landings from his command chair on the USS *Mount McKinley* lying offshore. Taking notes is Major-General E M Almond, X Corps commander. Nearest the camera is Brigadier-General Courtney Whitney, MacArthur's military secretary.

Katusas and troops arriving from the USA, it was still only at half strength for the landing. Of the 57 LSTs needed, the majority were found in Japan, acting as local harbor ferries, and were re-requisitioned back into the US Navy complete with their Japanese crews. Other small Japanese ships were employed as minesweepers by the Americans. So, only five years after Hiroshima, Japanese sailors were going to war in support of the United States, alongside the ROKA which itself contained many veterans of the Japanese Imperial forces.

As an exercise in staff planning and determination, Operation Chromite gleamed with brilliance. But it had also the characteristic MacArthur touch which tarnished its gleam. The logical choice to command the 1st Marine and 7th Divisions, grouped together as the US X Corps on 26 August, was Lieutenant-General Sheppard, and any appointment needed the prior approval of the JCS. Instead, without consulting the JCS, MacArthur appointed his own Chief-of-Staff, Major-General Edward Almond, who would command X Corps while retaining his staff position. Moreover, X Corps would not form part of Walker's EUSAK command but would act as a separate unit under MacArthur. The commander-in-chief himself would oversee the Inchon landing.

Already, on 17 August, MacArthur had again caused trouble for the government. In a letter to the Annual Convention of the Veterans of Foreign Wars he made some typically outspoken comments on the vital importance of Taiwan to Pacific security, at a time when Truman was trying to play down American commitment to Chiang Kai-shek. So great was MacArthur's reputation that the Secretary of Defense, Louis Johnson, at first refused to

LEFT: US Marines using scaling ladders to clear the harbor wall at Inchon.

BELOW LEFT: More Marines coming ashore at Inchon.

BOTTOM LEFT: Marines pushing forward from Inchon toward Seoul.

TOP RIGHT: Marines moving along the harbor wall to secure the port of Inchon.

BELOW: Men of the 1st Marine Division, supported by an M4A3 Sherman tank, secure Wolmi island.

BELOW RIGHT: Refugees in the area of Inchon.

send Truman's demand that MacArthur withdraw his letter. Finally, after much publicity, the letter was withdrawn and Johnson was replaced at Defense by General George C Marshall.

The preliminary moves for Operation Chromite began on 5 September as the first of 260 ships from seven nations under Vice-Admiral Struble left harbor in Japan, dodging a major typhoon that swept through the area. Meanwhile the Fifth Air Force attacked targets in the Seoul and Inchon area, and at 1230 hours on 13 September a combined US Navy and Royal Navy Gunfire Support Group arrived to bombard Wolmi-do, which was reduced to rubble in the next 36 hours, while other bombardments and deception landings took place on both coasts. With only about 3000 line-of-communications troops in the Seoul area there was little that the KPA could do. At 0633 on 15 September Wolmi-do was occupied virtually without loss by 3/5th Marines, and at 1730 that evening the rest of the 1st Marine Division assaulted the Inchon harbor wall. By 0200 the following morning the division was ashore and in secure positions for the loss of under 200 casualties. By the evening of the

19th it had advanced to the line of the River Han with the 7th Division landing to join it.

MacArthur now reinforced the Inchon perimeter with the ROK 1st Marine and 17th Regiments, and the US 187th Airborne RCT, which flew into Kimpo airfield near Seoul on 25 September. By this date the KPA defenders of the capital had increased to perhaps 20,000 troops, including elements of the 9th Division, the newly formed 18th and 25th Divisions, and even the 1st Air Division, a composite force made up of KPA ground crews. Meanwhile back at Pusan Lieutenant-General Walker had reorganized his EUSAK command in preparation for its

ABOVE: US Marines
escorting KPA prisoners
taken in the battle for Seoul.
Korean prisoners were
normally deprived of their
uniforms to prevent hidden
weapons being carried.

LEFT: Four of the crucial
LSTs unloading supplies at
Inchon harbor.

LEFT: A surprisingly
domestic scene as Marines
carrying ammunition press
ahead up the road from
Inchon to Seoul.

RIGHT: Dispirited North
Koreans captured in the
aftermath of the Inchon
landings.

own assault. On the 13th the US I Corps (1st Cavalry Division, 24th Division, ROKA 1st Division, British 29th Brigade) was activated, and three days later began a major offensive across the Naktong.

At first the KPA Front resisted strongly, but by 19 September, with its supply lines firmly cut by X Corps, it started to crumble. By the 23rd, as Walker activated the US IX Corps (2nd and 24th Divisions), the enemy was in headlong retreat from the perimeter. Three days later the 1st Cavalry Division, driving up from the south, linked up with the 7th Division at Osan, the original starting point for Task Force Smith almost three months before. Major-General Almond then put in a full X Corps attack against the KPA forces in Seoul, and by the 28th, after some bitter fighting, the ruined city fell. On the following day MacArthur – without consulting Truman or the JCS – formally restored Seoul to Syngman Rhee as President of the Republic of Korea. The ROK government, in its turn, took an ugly revenge on all those judged to have collaborated with the North Koreans.

Even before Chromite, MacArthur had raised the issue of the 38th Parallel with the JCS, and in the euphoria following his success even Truman's government seems to have lost sight of its original war aims. On 27 September the JCS informed MacArthur that his military objective was the destruction of the North Korean forces, and authorized the United Nations Command (UNC) to conduct ground, amphibious or airborne operations north of the 38th Parallel if necessary, on condition that no air operations took place near or across the Chinese or Soviet borders, none but ROKA troops advanced into the border provinces, and American troops were only to cross the frontier provided that 'there has been no entry into North Korea by major Soviet or Chinese Communist forces, no announcement of intended entry, nor a threat to counter our operations militarily in North Korea.'

On this basis, MacArthur ordered EUSAK to continue the advance from Seoul, with US I Corps on the left, US IX Corps in the center and ROKA II Corps (6th, 7th and 8th Divisions) on the right making the farthest advance. On 1 October, as MacArthur publicly demanded unconditional surrender from the North Korean forces, the ROKA 3rd Division was first across the frontier, followed by the rest of the ROKA forces. MacArthur also ordered X Corps to be taken by ship from Inchon to make a second amphibious landing on the east coast at Wonsan (Operation Tailboard). This attempt to repeat Inchon turned into a fiasco as the ROKA I Corps (3rd and Capitol

BELOW LEFT: ROKA soldiers rounding up KPA and suspected guerrilla prisoners after the recapture of Seoul, while M26 Pershing tanks of the US 1st Marine Division continue the advance, September 1950.

RIGHT: American troops of EUSAK moving up from the Pusan perimeter to link up with X Corps, September 1950.

BELOW: Korea was the first war to see extensive use of helicopters for casualty evacuation. This is a Sikorski S-51 of the US Marine Corps.

Divisions), advancing up the east coast, liberated Wonsan on 10 October, nine days before the Marines arrived offshore and 16 days before they could land.

By this time Kim Il Sung's once powerful Korean People's Army was in ruins. The Americans and ROKs claimed to have inflicted 200,000 casualties and taken 135,000 prisoners by the end of November, some being KPA verterans, others untrained conscripts caught up in the war's shifting fortunes. Many KPA troops moved into the hills to join the guerrilla war, and it is possible that the highest-ranking North Korean prisoner, Colonel Li Hak Ku, deliberately surrendered in order to organize resistance among prisoners of war at Koje island camp. What is certain is that the KPA never again mounted another offensive by itself. By the end of the

year it had reformed Chinese-style into five armies, each numbering no more than 20,000 men, the equivalent of a strong division. The ROKA was still a fragile organization, its casualties since the start of the war were at least 50,000, the majority 'missing.' Total EUSAK casualties were 24,172, including 3500 casualties suffered during the capture of Seoul. By this time the training and equipment problems which had afflicted American forces were close to being solved. Congress had increased the defense budget from $13 billion to over $50 billion a year, and something like 250,000 trained and equipped combat troops were on their way to MacArthur's command.

The Soviet Union was content to supply North Korea with military hardware, and to disrupt the further

workings of the UN Security Council. But in China Mao Tse-tung's government viewed MacArthur's advance with alarm. North Korea formed an essential part of the Manchurian industrial complex, for which the dams and hydroelectric plants on the Yalu River supplied about 10 percent of the power. The People's Republic of China was barely a year old, and having a hostile united Korea along its frontier on the Yalu was simply too great a threat. The difficulty was how to convey this simple message, through all the noisy rhetoric of the Cold War, to a nation with which Communist China had no diplomatic relations.

On 3 October Chou En-lai, the Chinese Prime Minister, summoned the Indian ambassador to Peking, K M Panikkar, to inform him that if American, as opposed to ROKA, troops crossed the 38th Parallel then China would enter the war. Pannikar duly relayed this threat, which MacArthur dismissed as 'pure bluff.' Others, particularly the British, took it more seriously, and began to sound warnings in Washington. All that summer, the Chinese PLA had been reinforcing Manchuria, and estimates put their strength there as high as 700,000 troops. Nevertheless, on 9 October EUSAK and X Corps on MacArthur's orders began a general advance northward across the 38th Parallel. On the same day the JCS authorized MacArthur to engage any Chinese forces in North Korea 'as long as in your judgment action by forces under your control offers a reasonable chance of success.' Meanwhile, American air raids close to the Manchurian border (and according to the Chinese, across it) continued.

Blocked in the UN Security Council by the Soviet veto, the United States now sought to maintain international support for the Korean War by transferring the debate to the General Assembly. Unlike the Security Council, every member state of the UN is represented in the General Assembly by one vote, and a two-thirds majority only is required to pass a resolution on 'important matters.' In 1950, the United States could virtually guarantee to find such a majority. On 7 October the General Assembly adopted Resolution 376(V), which recommended 'the establishment of a unified, independent and democratic Korea' and that 'all appropriate steps be taken to ensure conditions of stability throughout Korea,' so effectively removing the 38th Parallel as a war aim. The same resolution also created a new body, the United Nations Commission for the Unification and Rehabilitation of Korea (UNCURK), to replace UNCOK. In response to continued Soviet harassment and protest, the General Assembly went further, and on 3 November adopted Resolution 377(V), the historic and controversial 'Uniting For Peace' resolution, which states that if the Security Council fails through deadlock to achieve its primary purpose of maintaining peace, then the General Assembly may take over this function for itself.

American congressional elections were due in November 1950, and President Truman decided on a formal meeting with General MacArthur. Remarkably, the two men had never met before, MacArthur having served in the Far East since 1938, and such were the tensions and political complications involved that this public relations exercise turned almost into a state visit, with Wake Island in the Pacific being chosen as neutral territory. There, on 15 October, MacArthur assured Truman that the Communist Chinese would not dare interfere in the

war, that if they did FEAF airpower would slaughter them, and that the war would end in a month. MacArthur returned to Korea just in time to watch the capture of the North Korean capital of Pyongyang on the 20th by the 1st Cavalry Division, aided by a parachute drop by the 187th ARCT. Kim Il Sung's government fled to Sinuiji on the Yalu. Four days later MacArthur once again violated his orders. Despite JCS protests, he dropped all restrictions on non-ROKA forces and ordered all commanders 'to drive forward with all speed and full utilization of their forces.' Two days later, a platoon from the 7th Regiment, ROKA 6th Division, arrived at Chosan, the first UN troops to reach the Yalu.

Slightly earlier than this, three days after the Wake Island meeting, ROKA II Corps troops captured nine prisoners, the first of a steady trickle who claimed to have come from mainland China. But with all the exchanges

LEFT: Members of the ROK 5th Division and US 187 Airborne RCT pressing northward near Seoul, October 1950.

RIGHT: A wrecked T-34/85 tank abandoned by the KPA at Seoul, September 1950.

BELOW LEFT: American tankers keeping warm as the Korean winter approaches.

BELOW: One of the many bridges in Korea destroyed as the war moved up and down the country.

ABOVE: A US Navy F-4U Corsair waits to take off from the deck of the USS *Philippine Sea*, off the coast of Korea, October 1950.

LEFT: President Truman meets with General MacArthur on Wake Island, 15 October 1950.

ABOVE RIGHT: Men of 187 Airborne RCT jumping from a C-119 'Boxcar' transport aircraft.

RIGHT: The bodies of some of the many political prisoners killed by the KPA during their occupation of South Korea and discovered as UN forces advanced northward, October 1950.

LEFT: British Ferret and Daimler Scout armored cars used for long-range patrols in Korea.

BELOW LEFT: Troops of the ROK 5th Division pressing toward the Yalu, October 1950.

BOTTOM LEFT: An American soldier rests in a well dug-in position.

ABOVE RIGHT: Casualties arriving at a Mobile Army Surgical Hospital (MASH) unit in Korea.

RIGHT: Men of 187 Airborne RCT moving on foot up toward the Yalu, November 1950.

between the KPA and the PLA, there was nothing very unusual about Chinese among the North Korean forces, or North Koreans among the Chinese. Then, on 25 October, just as the ROKA's 6th DIvision reached the Yalu, sizeable Chinese forces emerged as if from nowhere to pounce upon the division, wrecking it and driving the other two divisions of the ROKA II Corps back in disorder. For a week, the whole ROKA line came under attack and its advance to the Yalu was stopped. Then the Chinese faded away as if they had never existed and by 5 November the front was again quiet.

It was hard to know what this sudden jolt could mean. In 1947 an investigation into Pearl Harbor had led to the foundation of a new Central Intelligence Agency (CIA) to prevent American forces ever again being surprised by an enemy attack. In October 1950, after the CIA had failed to predict the attack on South Korea, its head was replaced by Lieutenant-General Walter Bedell Smith, who had been Eisenhower's chief-of-staff in World War II. However, the highly professional American aerial photograph interpretation units of World War II had been disbanded in 1946, and the CIA was also short of funds. A handful of agents parachuted into the North came back with too little information, too late. MacArthur also made no secret of his contempt for the Chinese threat, seeing their intervention as an excuse to expand the war by striking at industrial Manchuria with his airpower. From early November he ordered FEAF to devastate the area immediately south of the Yalu, including the new capital of Sinuiju, which was bombed on the 8th.

By now the Korean winter, with temperatures 30 degrees below freezing, was hitting the mountains, and together with the Chinese threat this was enough to produce caution in many American units. On X Corps' front, the 1st Marine Division, joined by the British 41 Royal Marine Commando, left the US 3rd Division arriving at Hungnam and pushed slowly up to Chosin (Changjin) Reservoir. On 21 November American troops from the 17th Regiment, 7th Division, reached the Yalu at Hysanjin. With much reservation in Washington, EUSAK and X Corps, separated by 50 miles of guerrilla-infested mountains, began a general offensive on the 24th to end the war by Christmas. Totally unknown to them, they were advancing into a trap set with 200,000 Chinese troops.

Still hoping to avoid open involvement in a war with America, Mao had dispatched his forces to aid North Korea not as the official PLA but as the Chinese People's Volunteers or CPV (referred to by the Americans simply as the Chinese Communist Forces, or CCF). Notionally under the command of Kim Il Sung, their Chinese commander was Lin Piao, who as the PLA had no formal rank titles was officially known as *Yen-chan-chun Ssu-ling-*

yuan (Field Army Commanding Officer), commanding Fourth Field Army, made up of 13th Group Army (Thirty-eighth, Thirty-ninth and Fortieth Armies), the unattached Forty-second, Fiftieth and Sixty-sixth Armies, and 9th Group Army (Twentieth, Twenty-sixth and Twenty-seventh Armies) plus two artillery divisions.

A Chinese army was roughly equivalent to a reinforced Western division, and comprised three or sometimes four divisions, each of between 7000 and 10,000 men in three regiments of three battalions, plus an artillery battalion. Some were hardened from the wars against the Japanese and Kuomintang, others were former Kuomintang soldiers who had surrendered a year before,

ABOVE: Men of the 17th Regiment, US 7th Division, reach the Yalu River and the Chinese frontier, 21 November 1950.

LEFT: British troops of 1/Kings Own Scottish Borderers, 27th Infantry Brigade, fighting off a CPV attack, November 1950.

ABOVE RIGHT: A CPV attack begins.

ABOVE, FAR RIGHT: General MacArthur confers with Major-General John B Coulter, commanding US IX Corps, at his corps headquarters. Lieutenant-General Walker is on the far right, 24 November 1950.

RIGHT: CPV forces on the advance.

serving in what were virtually penal battalions. In keeping with Mao's ideas, the CPV was composed almost entirely of riflemen, with little artillery, armor, transport or support services. A division needed only 40 tons of supplies a day compared to 600 tons for an American division, and the use of about 700,000 human porters rather than road transport, with the troops moving only by night and hiding by day, had made possible a concentration as great as that of MacArthur's own forces in total secrecy. After three days of hammering in which ROKA II Corps, the farthest advanced EUSAK formation, was simply annihilated, the CPV went over to a general offensive on 27 November.

So began what American soldiers called 'The Big Bug-Out,' in which inexperienced ROKA and American units once more fell apart under surprise attack. In the west the US 2nd Division, joined by the 27th Commonwealth Brigade (so renamed by the addition of an Australian battalion) and the Turkish 1st Brigade became the rear-guard of a mass EUSAK retreat. In the east the 1st Marine Division decided to fight its way back through eight Chinese divisions, insisting with Marine pride that it was not retreating but advancing in a different direction. The epic retreat from 'Frozen Chosin' began on 1 December and ended in safety at Hungnam two weeks later. Under the umbrella of the Fifth Air Force,

Rear-Admiral Doyle evacuated the whole of X Corps and ROKA I Corps from east coast ports by Christmas Eve. Meanwhile on 5 December the Chinese had retaken Pyongyang, and on the 15th EUSAK was back behind the 38th Parallel having taken 13,000 casualties. By retreating 275 miles – the longest retreat in their history – the Americans had outrun the Chinese offensive, which had halted through supply difficulties and through its own massive casualties, which led 9th Group Army to withdraw to Manchuria to refit. To add to American problems, Lieutenant-General Walker was killed in a road accident close to the front on 23 December. His replacement commanding EUSAK, Lieutenant-General Matthew B Ridgway, arrived in Korea on the 26th to find 'bug-out fever' rife throughout his command.

In the next few weeks the shock of the unexpected Chinese offensive, and the possibility of American defeat, echoed around the world. A mention by Truman at a press conference on 30 November that America might conceivably use atomic bombs in Korea was enough to send British Prime Minister Clement Attlee racing to Washington by 4 December to argue for the original UN position of containment and limited war. On the same day the Army Chief of Staff, General J Lawton Collins, reached Tokyo to be told by MacArthur the staggering news that Seoul could not be saved or the ROKA relied upon, but that, if necessary, the old Pusan perimeter could be held by American troops indefinitely. On the 14th the UN General Assembly passed Resolution 384(V) calling for 'a satisfactory ceasefire in Korea' to be arranged as soon as possible. Eight days later Chou En-lai rejected this, announcing that the CPV would unify Korea by force. Already, on the 16th, President Truman had proclaimed a 'State of Emergency,' sending General Eisenhower to Europe with reinforcements for NATO. Opinion polls showed that a majority of Americans believed a third world war was about to start. On 31 December, as Ridgway struggled to restore order to EUSAK, the Chinese opened their New Year offensive to capture Seoul and destroy the UN forces for good.

One day before this General MacArthur presented to Washington his plan for winning the war. According to MacArthur, while American airpower destroyed the industrial centers of Manchuria and the US Navy blockaded the Chinese coast, Nationalist Chinese troops should be deployed both in Korea and in direct attacks on the Chinese mainland. These proposals went far beyond saving Korea, and were seen as an attempt to defeat Communist China and restore Chiang Kai-shek's Nationalists, and they could quite possibly have led to a third world war with the Soviet Union. On 9 January the JCS firmly rejected them, following up with letters from the JCS (12 January) and Truman (13 January) ordering MacArthur to fight even for the Korean islands if necessary, but to abandon the peninsula if it could not be held without excessive American casualties. Nothing daunted, MacArthur – so he later claimed – continued by requesting the atomic bombing of Manchuria, half a million Nationalist Chinese soldiers, and the laying of a belt of radioactive cobalt across the top of the Korean peninsula to prevent further CPV reinforcements, insisting that Korea could not otherwise be held.

The man who would prove MacArthur wrong was his own subordinate, Lieutenant-General Matthew

ABOVE: Troops of the
Turkish 1st Brigade falling
back across a frozen river, 6
December 1950.

RIGHT: US Marines wait to
continue their withdrawal
from Chosin with Chinese
prisoners in tow.

LEFT: The epic withdrawal
from Chosin by the 1st
Marine Division took place
in the face of massive
Chinese assaults.

Ridgway, former commander or airborne troops in Northwest Europe and Deputy Chief-of-Staff before his appointment to EUSAK. As the Chinese New Year offensive struck, Ridgway had in line from west to east US I Corps (3rd and 24th Divisions, the ROKA 1st Division, the Turkish 1st Brigade, and the British 29th Brigade); IX Corps (1st Cavalry Division, 25th Division, the ROK 6th Division, the British 27th Commonwealth Brigade, the Philippine 10th Battalion Combat Team, and Greek 1st Battalion); ROKA III Corps (2nd, 5th and 11th Divisions), the ROKA II Corps (6th, 7th and 8th Divisions). In immediate reserve was the 1st Marine Division, while the rest of X Corps and ROKA I Corps refitted at Pusan. Lin Piao, with 13th Group Army (Forty-second, Fiftieth and Sixty-sixth Armies, and KPA First and Fifth Armies facing the Americans, plus KPA Second, Third and Fourth Armies facing the ROKA went for what had always been the UN weakness: the gap in the line between the Americans and the ROKA caused by the Taebaek mountains. At the last minute, on 2 January, US X Corps (under EUSAK command since Ridgway's arrival) came back into line next to ROKA III Corps, but not in time to prevent its collapse. On the 4th, for the second time, communist forces occupied Seoul, and by the 24th Ridgway's line had been forced back a further 35 miles to just south of Osan, while, to the east, troops of the KPA's Second Army had infiltrated almost to within reach of Taegu, from where the Marines gradually repulsed them.

To restore the morale of EUSAK, Ridgway fell back upon the time-honored American method of insisting on a continuous front and letting the technology do the work in what he called 'The Meatgrinder' of American artillery and airpower. The newly arrived firepower, of which there was no longer a shortage, chewed up the lightly-armed CPV troops, more used to infiltration tactics than to direct attack against prepared enemy positions. On 15 January, in the very middle of the Chinese offensive, Ridgway ordered Operation Wolfhound, a probing attack by the 27th RCT ('the Wolfhounds') of the US 25th Division, which showed that the CPV was running out of steam.

It was now the Chinese turn to have bad luck: Lin Piao fell sick or was wounded, and was replaced in command of the CPV by Peng Teh-huai, who informed Mao that Korea could no longer be conquered by force. On the 25th Ridgway began Operation Thunderbolt, a slow-

ABOVE LEFT: A British Centurion tank, probably the best tank of the war, crossing an icy river, 3 January 1951.

LEFT: Two surrendering CPV soldiers.

ABOVE: American troops watch part of the 'Meatgrinder,' a white phosphorous bombardment.

RIGHT: Peng Teh-huai, on the left, pictured during the Korean War.

moving drive by I and IX Corps for the Han River, followed by Operation Punch by the 25th Division and Operation Roundup by X and ROKA III Corps on 5 February. On 21 February the clearly-named Operation Killer, a general offensive by IX and X Corps, began. By 1 March the CPV line on the Han had collapsed. A slow, deliberate American advance was coupled with an equally deliberate Chinese withdrawal, for which casualties can only be guessed. On 7 March Operation Ripper, the follow-up to Killer, got underway, and on the 14th Seoul changed hands once more, for the fourth time in nine months. This time considerable care was taken crossing the 38th Parallel. On 5 April EUSAK began its last offensive, Operation Rugged, which brought it to Line Kansas, a practical defensive line running a little north to south of the old frontier, by the 14th.

The strategy of limited war had now been fully adopted by Truman's government. As had been shown, the 38th Parallel was not practical either as a political or a military frontier, but a more defensible line close to it and a restored South Korea might become the basis of negotiation. Ridgway as Deputy Chief-of-Staff had himself been part of the process of forming this new war aim. 'We didn't set out to conquer China,' he told a press conference on 12 March, 'we set out to stop Communism.' The war aim of 'meeting Communist aggression' was adopted by the UN General Assembly as Resolution 498(V) on 1 February 1951, condemning China and North Korea as aggressors, and being followed (on 18 May) by Resolution 500(V) calling on those states which had not supplied troops to the UN Command to support the war with economic sanctions.

LEFT: Canadian soldiers of Princess Patricia's Light Infantry in Korea, February 1951.

BELOW: American soldiers surrendering to CPV forces. Although obviously posed, this picture reflects the substantial US losses during the CPV offensives of early 1951.

ABOVE: US Marines advancing past a captured enemy bunker during Operation Ripper.

ABOVE RIGHT: A Bofors anti-aircraft gun of the British 29th Infantry Brigade being used to support an attack on an enemy position south of Seoul, February 1951.

RIGHT: Troops of the ROK 6th Division, part of US IX Corps, during Operation Ripper.

General MacArthur, at his own press conference on 7 March, attacked what became known as this 'Die for Tie' strategy, which seemed to him to offer nothing but protracted war, mass casualties and stalemate. Finally, MacArthur overreached himself. Aware of a tentative peace proposal being worked out by Truman's government, he issued on 24 March his own public demand for a ceasefire based on the Chinese 'complete inability to accomplish by force of arms the conquest of Korea,' and the threat of UN attack on Manchuria which 'would doom Red China to the risk of imminent military collapse,' giving the Chinese little choice but to refuse angrily. Then, on 5 April, the Republican minority leader read to the House of Representatives a letter from MacArthur in which he once more raised the issue of Nationalist Chinese troops, and first used a phrase that,

repeated several times, showed his complete lack of sympathy with the government plan: 'There is no substitute for victory.'

Despite his immense political power and prestige, the MacArthur who had nearly bungled away his command on the Yalu seemed in Washington a very different figure from MacArthur the victor of Inchon. After a few days consulting with the military, with friends, and with the British to obtain support for his move, Truman dismissed MacArthur from his commands and on 11 April ordered his return to the United States. Due to an error in signaling, MacArthur learned of his dismissal at lunchtime in Tokyo from a commercial radio broadcast. It was an immensely sad end to such a career. 'He asked for it,' Truman explained to General Eisenhower, 'and I had to give it to him.'

THE ROAD TO PANMUNJON

On returning to the United States, MacArthur portrayed himself as an innocent patriot, victim of a government that was corrupt, unstable, and riddled with communists. Senator McCarthy and other prominent Republicans supported this view, including one future president, then Senator Richard Nixon of California, who observed that the 'happiest group in the country are the communists and their stooges.' Other Republicans called for President Truman's impeachment. Telegrams in support of MacArthur flooded into Washington and opinion polls showed that over two-thirds of the American people opposed his recall. At Republican invitation, MacArthur addressed both Houses of Congress on 19 April. In his deeply emotional style he argued that 'once war is forced upon us, there is no other alternative than to apply every available means to bring it to a swift end,' and that the idea of 'appeasing' Communist China was both dangerous and impractical. That afternoon he rode in triumphal procession through Washington, and next day in a second procession through New York watched by 7,500,000 people. On the 25th Congress voted to hold a formal enquiry into MacArthur's dismissal and the 'military situation in the Far East.'

The hearings began on 3 May. MacArthur, while not denying the president's right to dismiss him, argued that the notion of limited war 'seems to me to introduce a new concept into military operations — the concept of appeasement' and that 'to me, that would mean that you would have a continued and indefinite extension of bloodshed.' Dean Acheson as Secretary of State, General

Marshall as Secretary of Defense, and General Bradley as Chairman of the JCS all appeared before the hearings and dismissed MacArthur's ideas as out of date. As Bradley put it, 'the fundamental military issue which has arisen is whether to increase the risk of a global war by taking additional measures that are open to the United States and its allies.' The hearings ended on 17 August with little resolved. MacArthur's views were worth serious consideration, but were not worth a constitutional crisis.

Nevertheless, just as the Democrats had done badly out of the November 1950 congressional elections, so the split between MacArthur and Truman would hurt them in the forthcoming 1952 presidential election. The issue of limited war itself has never been resolved. The Truman Doctrine of containment at first proved very popular with American military and political theorists. As a result of Korea, the United States built up strong conventional forces in peacetime, prepared to fight in a wide variety of wars, with the appropriate level of force in each case, to contain the communist threat. But it has since

been argued that the notions of containment and defeating aggression developed in Korea, rather than allowing the military to fight for victory, were the forerunners of the hesitant and finally disastrous American strategy in Vietnam between 1961 and 1975. In 1984 President Ronald Reagan told a press conference that MacArthur should have been allowed 'to lead us to victory in Korea.'

Between MacArthur's dismissal and the start of the congressional hearings, the Chinese in Korea made two further attempts to break through the UN line and secure a military victory. General Ridgway, who had performed wonders in restoring the morale of EUSAK and leading it back from near disaster, was appointed to take over from MacArthur as CINCUNC, together with all MacArthur's other appointments. Ridgway generously retained Lieutenant-General Almond commanding X Corps while replacing him as chief-of-staff. His own replacement commanding EUSAK and all other UNC ground troops in Korea was Lieutenant-General James Van Fleet, who like Walker and Ridgway had commanded a corps in Northwest Europe, and who shared their belief in massed firepower. His demands for extra artillery shells and ammunition soon became known among army supply staffs in Korea as 'the Van Fleet Load.'

On 19 April, five days after he arrived in Korea, Van Fleet ordered US I Corps and IX Corps to push up past Line Kansas to Line Wyoming, partly inside the 'Iron Triangle,' the key communist supply and communications region lying east of the Imjin River between the towns of

PAGES 58-59: South Korean refugees fleeing from a communist offensive.

ABOVE LEFT: Dean Acheson, Truman's Secretary of State, addressing the UN, November 1951.

BELOW LEFT: General MacArthur's parade through New York City, 20 April 1951.

BELOW: Men of the 25th Infantry Division on 'Heartbreak Ridge,' 1951.

Chorwon, Kumhwa and Pyonggang (not to be confused with Pyongyang, the North Korean capital). Predictably, after dusk on 22 April, Peng Teh-huai struck back in what the CPV counted as its 'First Step, Fifth Phase Offensive,' but is generally known as the 'First Communist Spring Offensive,' the largest offensive of the war. For this, the Chinese had assembled 30 divisions in the first wave and 40 in reserve – more than 500,000 men. The 3rd Group Army and 19th Group Army (including the KPA First Army) struck between the Imjin and the coast in a drive on Seoul, while 9th Group Army and 13th Group Army attacked from the other side of the Iron Triangle in a large pincer movement. The KPA Second, Third and Fifth Armies launched holding attacks in the east. Van Fleet's deployment had the US I Corps covering the west coast, then US IX Corps, US X Corps, ROKA I Corps and ROKA III Corps. As a matter of policy ROKA divisions were included in American corps, and on this occasion the ROKA 6th Division collapsed, leaving a gaping hole in the IX Corps' line. Van Fleet promptly began an orderly retreat of 30 miles, covered by artillery and airpower, to the Hongchon River, a position humorously designated as the 'No-Name Line.'

During this retreat a miniature epic of heroism took place on the Imjin as the British 29th Brigade (three battalions plus the Belgian 1st Battalion) held off the Third Army's main thrust, the four divisions of the Sixty-third Army, inflicting 11,000 casualties on the enemy in three days before being forced back. Of the brigade rearguard,

1/Gloucestershire Regiment ('the Glosters'), only 63 men reached safety, so adding 'Gloster Hill' to the list of British battle honors marking where small units have overcome impossible odds. Van Fleet himself described Gloster Hill as 'the most outstanding example of unit bravery in modern warfare.' Typically, the British chose afterward to make a joke of it. 'When Tom told corps that his position was "a bit sticky,"' recalled one brigade officer, 'they simply did not grasp that in British Army parlance, that meant "critical."' Thanks to the stand of the 29th Brigade, the US I Corps was able to retire safely to No-Name Line by 29 April. In the process of withdrawal, EUSAK, together with FEAF, inflicted 70,000 casualties on the enemy in return for 7000 of its own, leaving a 10-mile strip of devastated countryside between the two forces.

Van Fleet at once ordered a methodical advance back northwards. Although the Americans came forward cautiously, the ROKs to the east pushed ahead, and were actually north of the old Line Kansas by 10 May, with the whole UN line pivoting forward on the west coast anchor of the US I Corps. The redeployment of the CPV's 3rd Group Army with 9th Group Army in the east, next to KPA fifth Army and second Army, now made it clear that Peng would attack along the spine of the Taebaek mountains. Although aimed at the main ROKA forces, which had proved less reliable than the Americans, this was an act of desperation. Not even a Chinese offensive could be maintained and supplied in such broken

LEFT: American infantry of the 25th Division hitching a ride on M4 Sherman tanks during the retreat to the 'No-Name Line.'

RIGHT: American soldiers surrendering to CPV troops.

BELOW RIGHT: An officer of the Glosters pointing out Gloster Hill after the battle.

BELOW: The 187 ARCT making one more combat jump during Van Fleet's counterattack from the 'No-Name Line.'

country. The 'Second Step, Fifth Phase Offensive,' or 'Second Spring Offensive,' began late on 15 May, and the ROKA III Corps (which was later disbanded) once more broke and collapsed, leaving US X Corps with its flank in the air. Van Fleet switched the US 3rd Division and the 187th ARCT across from I Corps to bolster X Corps, while once more falling back to what was now the 'Modified No-Name Line.' In four days the communist offensive was smashed with the loss of 90,000 men.

These battles confirmed the American experience of World Wars I and II: hordes of unsupported riflemen, however brave, could not break through a defense based on superior firepower from artillery and the air. The fighting since April had cost the CPV at least 200,000 casualties, and temporarily its will to fight was broken. As the Americans once more moved forward on 18 May they found that for the first time in the war Chinese troops were surrendering in large numbers.

Once again, the Americans had the option of driving the enemy back all the way to the Yalu. This time, they carefully declined this option. At a National Security Council meeting in Washington on 16 May it was decided that, while the political aim of the United States remained 'a unified, independent, democratic Korea,' the military aim should be to secure a line 'suitable for defense and administration and not substantially below the 38th Parallel.' The line finally selected was Line Wyoming, including the base of the Iron Triangle. In Operation Piledriver EUSAK forces pushed up to Pyonggang by 13 June, only to fall back four days later. Van Fleet then ordered the fortification of his line, now dubbed the Main Line of Resistance (MLR).

This deliberate move by EUSAK could hardly have been more clear. The Americans were not fighting to win a war but to signal a diplomatic message: the Chinese could not conquer South Korea, while the Americans themselves had no interest in conquering North Korea. This policy was reinforced by a Senate Resolution of 17 May calling for an armistice on the 38th Parallel, and by an announcement on 1 June by the UN Secretary General that such an armistice would satisfy the original Security Council Resolution 1501 under which the UN had gone to war. On the 23rd the Soviet ambassador to the UN, in an informal broadcast on the UN radio

ABOVE: Soviet Deputy Foreign Minister Malik on UN Radio on 26 June 1951 repeating Soviet hints of a peaceful settlement made by the Soviet ambassador three days beforehand.

LEFT: The communist delegation to Kaesong: Generals Hsieh Fang and Teng Hua of the CPV, Nam Il, Lee Sang Cho and Chang Pyong San of the KPA.

RIGHT: US troops of the 2nd Infantry Division on the Main Line of Resistance.

station, suggested armistice negotiations between the two sides in Korea. With the ground well prepared, Ridgway was authorized on 29 June to offer the start of such negotiations. These were to be military negotiations with the intention of ending the fighting, not a political discussion on the future of Korea. Kim Il Sung for the KPA and Peng Teh-huai for the CPV accepted this invitation, stipulating that the location should be the town of Kaesong, lying between the opposing forces.

Talks began on 10 July, with the American delegation expecting to conclude an armistice in three to six weeks. The one force not represented was the ROKA. Syngman Rhee felt himself betrayed by the American decision and continued to insist on a unified democratic Korea, refusing to take part in the talks. The Americans soon found, however, that they had another problem. Kaesong was three miles south of the 38th Parallel, and firmly in communist hands. Every effort was made to portray the American delegation as coming to surrender, and as recognizing the governments of communist China and North Korea. By 22 August the talks had broken down.

In response to this breakdown, Ridgway allowed Van Fleet to conduct further limited offensives to improve his position on the MLR. The first, lasting from 26 August to 14 October, was to push the communist forces back from Height 1211, dominating the Hwachon reservoir. Against heavy opposition the Marines, US soldiers and ROKs of X Corps took 6400 casualties in securing the heights, which they renamed 'Bloody Ridge' and 'Heartbreak Ridge.' On 3 October US I Corps also pushed forward to improve its position in Operation Commando, fighting for a prominent hill known as 'Old Baldy' which would change hands several times in the war. By the 19th the position had been secured for the loss of 4000 casualties, the majority from the 1st Cavalry Division, which was finally withdrawn from Korea and replaced by the 45th (Oklahoma National Guard) Division. The fighting from August to October had cost the UNC 60,000 casualties including 22,000 Americans, bringing the number of American casualties in the war to over 100,000. American estimates of communist casualties ran as high as 234,000. They were at least enough for the CPV and KPA to agree to a resumption of talks at

Panmunjon, just east of Kaesong and genuinely in no-man's land, on 25 October.

The American position regarding any armistice negotiations was still surprisingly close to MacArthur's view of war – that once a clear military decision had been reached, armed activity should cease and swift discussions begin to end the conflict. Unfortunately they did not realize that the Chinese communist view was completely different. The Marxist-Leninist philosophy of both Mao Tse-tung and Kim Il Sung held that what was important was the political result, and that armed force and negotiations were just tools to secure that result, so both might run side by side together. This, added to the belief of communists everywhere in their political superiority and to the Chinese belief in their own cultural superiority, made negotiating with them a frustrating experience for the Americans, who viewed themselves as representatives of the greatest power on earth. 'The United Nations command delegation has been in search of an expression,' the American chief negotiator told his opposite number on 11 August, 'which conveys the haughty intransigence, the arbitrary inflexibility, and the unreasoning stubbornness of your attitude.' His successor was to compare the CPV approach to that of 'common criminals.'

An example of how little the Americans understood the Chinese and North Koreans came on 31 October when the communists agreed for the first time to a demarkation line for the armistice based on the MLR. In response, Ridgway instructed Van Fleet that he could no longer mount an operation of more than battalion size (1000 men) without permission from CINCUNC headquarters. On 17 November the Americans at Panmunjon proposed that the MLR should constitute the armistice line provided that the armistice was signed within 30 days, and on the 27th this agreement was ratified. To the Americans it looked like the end of the war. In fact they had handed the communists a 30-day ceasefire, which they used to improve their positions along the MLR, constructing 77 miles of tunnels and 3427 miles of trenches

FAR LEFT: US infantry of the 38th Division digging in on 'Old Baldy.'

RIGHT: North Korean and American negotiators at Panmunjon.

BELOW LEFT: An American flamethrower burning out a communist strongpoint.

BELOW LEFT: Generals Ridgway (right) and Van Fleet (center with cap) with Vice-President Barkley and Brigadier-General T J Cross, Korea, November 1951.

BELOW: An American Quad .50-caliber machine-gun.

BELOW RIGHT: An 8-inch howitzer prepares to fire.

in a defensive system 14 miles deep and 155 miles long from coast to coast. They then allowed the 30-day time-limit to run out.

This episode marked the end of major ground fighting in Korea, but not the end of the war. This would continue, together with the Panmunjon negotiations, for another 20 months, with the MLR never moving more than 10 miles in either direction. With American and Western war production running at full strength, Van Fleet had 229,000 American troops in Korea and 357,000 ROKs and other UNC contingents, of which the largest was the British 1st Commonwealth Division. Formed on 28 July 1951, this comprised the 28th Commonwealth Brigade (the renamed 27th Brigade), the 29th Brigade and the Canadian 25th Brigade, with a New Zealand artillery regiment. Thailand sent its 21st Regiment, Ethiopia its 1st Kanew Battalion ('the Conquerors'), while France, the Netherlands and Columbia each sent a composite infantry battalion, and Denmark, India, Italy, Norway and Sweden sent medical units. The

final line-up of UN forces on the MLR became the US I Corps holding the west coast, then the US IX Corps, the ROKA II Corps, the US X Corps, and the ROKA I Corps, together making up EUSAK. On the far side of the MLR, Peng Teh-huai grouped his CPV forces in the west and center of the country, leaving the east to the KPA, all deployed with about half their forces in reserve at any one time. The total number of troops was about 90 divisions, or 700,000 men.

This controlled stalemate on the ground was made possible by total American dominance of the sea and air, enabling them to isolate the peninsula and preventing any communist attempt to land troops behind the MLR. On 3 April 1951 the US Navy and Royal Navy blockading forces were placed, under the US Seventh Fleet as Task Force 95 (for operational purposes), consisting of Task Group 95.1, a chiefly Royal Navy light carrier group in the Yellow Sea, and Task Group 95.2, a larger mixed force to cover the Sea of Japan. Providing support to the land battle was Task Force 77, four American fleet aircraft carriers and their escorts operating in the Sea of Japan. So complete was UN control of the sea that North Korean ports could be 'besieged' by American battleships. Between 16 February 1951 and 27 July 1953 Wonsan was reduced to rubble by the longest siege in American naval history, while Hungnam and Sagjim endured similar fates. Amphibious raids on a small scale were also made on the North Korean coast. In late 1951 a plan was drawn up for a major amphibious landing north of the MLR, but canceled by General Bradley.

The war in the air was not quite as one-sided. Just as the appearance of CPV forces on the Yalu startled EUSAK in October 1950, so on 1 November a shock occurred when a flight of F-51 Mustangs was buzzed over the Yalu by six single-seat swept-wing jet interceptors with Chinese markings. These were Mikoyan-Gurevich MiG-15s, the very latest in Soviet technology supplied to the Chinese, and based at the Antung complex in Manchuria just north of the Yalu. On the 8th a flight of MiG-15s engaged USAF F-80 Shooting Stars over the Yalu in the first ever jet-versus-jet combat, in which Lieutenant Russell Brown USAF became the first jet pilot in history to shoot down another jet.

The American response to the MiG-15 was to send their own fast jet interceptor, the F-86 Sabre, to Korea. Based for most of the war at Kimpo airfield near Seoul, the 4th Fighter-Interceptor Wing (joined in February 1952 by the 51st Fighter-Interceptor Wing) of Sabres fought a war seemingly remote from the rest of Korea, engaging the MiGs in single combat at 50,000 feet over the Yalu. In fact they were performing the vital service of maintaining air superiority. Without the Sabres, the MiG-15s could have raided South Korea at low altitude against the UN bombers, fighter-bombers, and transport aircraft that provided essential support for the ground troops. The Chinese and North Korean MiG-15 pilots, trained by Soviet advisors, were no match for the vastly more experienced Americans. In the course of the war the Sabres claimed 757 confirmed kills compared to

TOP: Supermarine Seafires of the Fleet Air Arm on HMS *Triumph*.

ABOVE: A North Korean Illushin Il-2 being shot down by a F-51 Mustang of 18th Fighter-Bomber Wing, 20 June 1951.

LEFT: The aircraft carrier USS *Antietam* and the battleship USS *Wisconsin* being replenished at sea.

ABOVE RIGHT: A USAF F-80 Shooting Star based on a temporary airstrip in South Korea.

RIGHT: The battleship USS *Missouri* bombarding enemy shore positions.

RIGHT: ROKA infantry on the Main Line of Resistance.

BELOW RIGHT: A Douglas B-26 Invader medium bomber of the 3rd Bomber Wing during Operation Strangle.

BOTTOM RIGHT: B-29 Superfortresses release their bombloads over Korea.

LEFT: An F-86 Sabre in flight over Korea.

BELOW LEFT: 40mm guns on the USS Missouri firing on targets in North Korea.

103 of their own aircraft lost, while 39 pilots made 'Ace' by shooting down five enemy aircraft or more. The first man to make 'Jet Ace' was Captain James Jabara on 20 May 1951, and the highest scorer for the war was Captain Joseph McConnell Jr with 16 kills. The chief frustration suffered by Sabre pilots was that the enemy, if hit, could retire north of the Yalu, where the Americans were forbidden to fly in recognition of the fiction that China was not actually at war.

Protected by the Sabres, the UN air forces wrecked virtually every major city in North Korea in three years, just as had been predicted. In addition to British Fleet Air Arm aircraft, the Australians and South Africans each contributed one fighter squadron, but the overwhelming might of airpower in Korea was American – a total of 4000 aircraft in use by the end of the war. On 23 June 1952 the Americans for the first time used B-29s to bomb the Yalu dams which supplied North Korea with most of its electricity, and followed this up in summer by reducing Pyongyang to rubble.

As an aid to the ground troops the aircraft were absolutely essential, but the US Air Force still clung to its belief that airpower by itself could win a war. Between June 1951 and June 1952 it tried, together with navy and Marines aircraft to force a communist retreat from the MLR by cutting off their supplies, bombing and shooting at ground transport and communications along a 100-mile belt just north of the 38th Parallel in Operation Strangle. In fact, although massively destructive to North Korea itself, this had little effect on the CPV and KPA. While static in entrenchments they needed only 3000 tons of supplies daily which could be brought forward by human porters.

The remaining American option to end the war was to

use atomic weapons. Truman's observations on 30 November 1950 were the closest the United States came publicly to threatening atomic war, but the matter was sometimes discussed by the JCS and by Truman's government. The nature of the argument was changed sharply during the Korean War by two developments. In January 1951 the Americans tested a tactical atomic weapon, small enough to fit into an artillery shell and practical for use on the battlefield. Then, on 1 November

1952, the Americans tested a hydrogen or thermonuclear bomb, with an explosive force several hundred times that of an atomic weapon. A thermonuclear third world war could, quite literally, destroy all life on the planet. The Soviet Union tested a thermonuclear device a year later.

At the other end of the scale, the guerrilla war in South Korea took a savage turn between November 1951 and December 1952 with Operation Ratkiller, a sustained

ABOVE: Some of the 21 Americans who refused repatriation, wearing Chinese uniforms at Panmunjon, 29 January 1953.

LEFT: North Korean POWs in American custody.

RIGHT: Wounded of the US 2nd Infantry Division receive attention. Note the ROKA scout with the patrol.

attempt by ROKA troops to wipe out the guerrilla threat completely. By the end of January 1952 about 20,000 people had been killed or imprisoned, compared to an estimated total guerrilla strength of 30,000, but the trouble continued through to the end of the year. Exactly how many of those imprisoned were actually guerrillas cannot be estimated. By the end of the war Syngman Rhee's government had become the custodian of camps containing 132,000 prisoners of war (POWs), including KPA and CPV soldiers, guerrillas, and probably a very large number of confused and innocent people.

The legal position of both sides at Panmunjon on POWs was based on Article 118 of the 1949 Geneva Convention, which states that 'prisoners of war shall be released and repatriated without delay after the cessation of hostilities.' In fact, the United States had signed the Convention, but not yet ratified it, and neither Communist China nor North Korea had signed it, but all agreed to observe its provisions. In the American view, first stated on 18 February, a significant number of the POWs held in South Korea camps were neither North Koreans nor communists, and provisional lists showed that only 70,000 or so wanted to return 'home' to the North or to China. The communist delegation could not accept this, and on 7 May the two sides announced publicly that the issue of POW repatriation was the only thing preventing a ceasefire being finalized along the line of the MLR.

The treatment of POWs on both sides also became a major issue of the Korean War. In the war's first phase neither KPA nor ROKA troops in combat showed any reluctance to shoot prisoners out of hand, and while American, UN and CPV troops often behaved better, there were many exceptions. The POW camps run by the ROKA were overcrowded, unhygienic and subject to frequent riots. On American estimates, 6600 prisoners died in UN custody during 1951. The camp on Koje island soon degenerated into a lawless commune organized and administered by the prisoners themselves. On 8 May 1952, in a notorious incident, the prisoners on Koje actually captured the American camp commandant and held him for three days.

On the other side, of 7140 American prisoners of the North Koreans and Chinese, 2701 died in POW camps, together with 50 out of 1188 Commonwealth POWs. Conditions in the camps were harsh, and there were many cases of physical abuse and torture. Much of the suffering, however, came from what might be called 'culture shock.' Many American soldiers captured in the early part of the war had come to Korea virtually untrained, without the morale and self-discipline necessary for survival. What to the Chinese were poor living conditions and short rations were desolation and starvation to these men, and deaths were reported as due to 'give-upitis,' first cousin to the 'bug-out fever' that affected EUSAK in December 1950. UN troops from less developed countries, such as the Colombians and the Turks, adjusted far better and suffered no deaths in captivity.

The Chinese operated a cruel system of rewards and punishments intended to win over their captives, the same methods which they had used to 're-educate' prisoners from the Kuomintang Army to fight for them after 1949. In response to persistent pressure from their captors the majority of POWs did what was necessary for survival, but about 13 percent of all American POWs became outright collaborators. Twenty-one Americans and one Briton, together with 325 Koreans, became converts to communism, preferring to stay rather than return home after the war. This was too much for the CIA, which became convinced that the Chinese used sophisticated drug-based mind control techniques, and would spend the rest of the decade looking for them. More sensibly, in 1955 the US Armed Forces issued the Uniform Code of Conduct, setting out the behavior expected of an American prisoner of war.

Central to the brainwashing scare was the communist claim in February and March 1952 that the United States had begun large scale biological warfare, spreading anthrax, cholera and other diseases over North Korea. This claim was supported by confessions from American POWs admitting to being involved in germ warfare. After the war the Americans went to great lengths to show that these confessions were either forgeries or the product of brainwashing. It is known that the United States – along with many other countries – was experimenting with germ warfare at the time of Korea, and there is just enough circumstantial evidence to allow the Chinese claim to be taken seriously. What robs it of credibility is its timing. Coming as a major accusation against the Americans, just as the Panmunjon talks on prisoners stalled, the accusation seemed a little too obvious to be true.

Through 1952 the stalemated war dragged on, with its steady drain of casualties, producing increasing discontent in the United States. The presidential election was due in the autumn, with Truman refusing to stand for a third term, and how different Korea was from war as MacArthur understood it was shown when the CPV joined in the electoral process. On 6 October, with the presidential campaign in its last stages, they launched their biggest attack since Heartbreak Ridge against the US I and IX Corps. Van Fleet's response was to mount Operation Showdown, an attempt to drive the Chinese back which began on the 14th, but resulted only in the

capture of three hills for the cost of 8000 casualties. The lesson was not lost on the American public. Adlai Stevenson, the Democratic candidate, lost in a landslide to the strongest candidate the Republicans could field, General Dwight D Eisenhower, who had promised a complete re-assessment of the war. Eisenhower's victory meant a change of attitude and personnel. Already General Ridgway had been promoted and moved to NATO in April 1952. His successor as CINCFE and CINCUNC was General Mark Clark, who had commanded the US Fifth Army in Italy in World War II and had a reputation for political skill. At the same time, the Americans restored Japanese self-government and abolished the post of SCAP.

Eisenhower's policy for ending the war was to threaten direct action whenever the armistice talks stalled, advising the North Koreans on 14 December 1952 that the United States would strike against them in future 'under circumstances of our own choosing.' Once more the president and the JCS discussed ways of using atomic weapons in Korea. On 2 February 1953 Eisenhower announced that the Seventh Fleet would no longer prevent Nationalist Chinese attacks from hitting Communist China. On the 11th General Van Fleet was replaced as commander of EUSAK by Lieutenant-General Maxwell D Taylor, who had led an airborne division under

ABOVE: General Mark Clark (far left) with General Ridgway and Admiral Turner Joy in Korea, May 1952.

LEFT: A Sikorski S-51 helicopter carries wounded to the 8063rd MASH (Mobile Army Surgical Hospital).

ABOVE RIGHT: Another casualty reaching a MASH unit. The helicopter is a Bell H-13D.

RIGHT: 'Old Baldy' visible from American positions.

Ridgway in World War II and who was committed to a policy of holding American losses down while building up the ROKA to take over a greater share of the fighting.

Now came probably the most crucial event: the death of Stalin on 5 March 1953. Ten days later his successor, Georgi Malenkov, announced that 'there is no disputed or unresolved question that cannot be settled peacefully,' and things began to happen very quickly indeed. On 6 April the communist negotiators at Panmunjon reversed their position and agreed to voluntary repatria-

tion. The first phase, Operation Little Switch, began at Panmunjon itself on the 20th when 700 CPV and 5100 KPA troops were exchanged for 450 KOKs and 150 other UN troops. True to their beliefs, however, the Chinese tried to obtain the best possible negotiating position by increasing ground attacks along the MLR. Small hills like Old Baldy and Pork Chop Hill, scene of a magnificent defense by the US 31st Regiment between 16 and 18 April, became major political tests between the two sides.

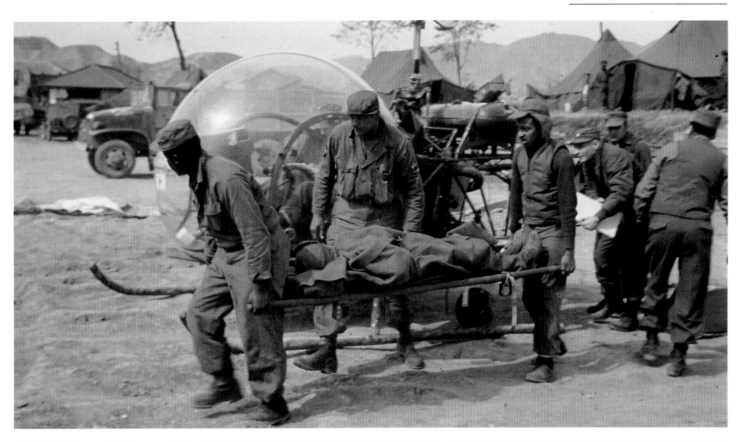

Casualties among UN troops were 4343 in April and 7570 in May as the Chinese, losing about twice as many themselves, increased the pressure. The United States retaliated by bombing, between 13 and 16 May, the five main irrigation dams on the Yalu on which the North Korean rice crop depended, causing untold flood damage and crippling the country's economy. On the 16th in a message intended for Mao Tse-tung, Eisenhower's Secretary of State, John Foster Dulles, told President Nehru of India that the United States would use the

atomic bomb in Korea if necessary.

The one government that still did not want peace in Korea was the Republic of Korea itself under Syngman Rhee, who continued to insist that the Americans had betrayed him. On 25 May all sides at Panmunjon accepted a modified version of UN General Assembly Resolution 610(VII) of 3 December 1952, whereby prisoners of war who refused repatriation should be passed to a Neutral National Reparations Commission (NNRC) supervised by India. President Rhee's rage at this was so great that Eisenhower seriously considered using Plan Ever-Ready, a contingency plan to depose him and seize control of the South Korean government. On 10 June, as a political signal, the Chinese launched the biggest offensive on the MLR for two years against ROKA II Corps, driving it back three miles in a week. On 18 June President Rhee tried ingeniously to sabotage the armistice negotiations by ordering ROKA troops to release all POWs. About 25,000 escaped, despite American attempts to recapture them. On 12 July Rhee was pressured into accepting the terms of the armistice in return for military aid and a postwar alliance with the United States. This agreement came just too late to prevent a final communist offensive, aimed specifically at the ROKA, which opened on the 13th and caused about 25,000 casualties to each side in a week.

Despite Rhee's efforts, the armistice ending the fighting in Korea was signed at Panmunjon by Kim Il Sung for the KPA, Peng Teh-huai for the CPV and Mark Clark for the United Nations Command on 27 July 1953. The ROKA did not sign the armistice, and has never done so. Operation Big Switch, the final exchange of prisoners, started on 5 August, with 75,823 prisoners being returned North and 22,604 to the NNRC by the UN troops. In return, the communists gave back 12,773 prisoners to the UN and 359 to the NNRC, The UN General Assembly expressed by Resolution 712(VII) of 28 August its 'profound satisfaction that fighting has now ceased in Korea on the basis of an honorable armistice.'

Of 1,319,000 Americans who served in Korea 33,629 were killed and a further 105,785 wounded. Nearly half the American casualties were suffered after the opening of armistice negotiations. British Commonwealth losses were 1263 killed and 4817 wounded. The Turkish brigade lost about 900 dead and 3500 wounded, and the remaining eight other UN contingents about the same number. Published estimates of ROKA dead range from 47,000 to 415,000. In fact, ROKA and South Korean civilian losses can only be guessed at. The same is true of KPA, CPV and North Korean civilian casualties, although between them they must run into millions.

An armistice is still, in international law, a state of war. The Korean armistice was to have been overtaken by a peace conference beginning in October 1953. This in fact took until April 1954 to meet in Geneva, and failed to reach any agreement. Neither Korean state has ever

RIGHT: Mark Clark watches the exchange of prisoners at Panmunjon, May 1953. Lieutenant-General Maxwell Taylor is far left, with paratrooper wings on his tunic.

BELOW LEFT: A 31st Infantry Regiment outpost on 'Old Baldy' on the day the Korean Armistice was signed, 27 July 1953.

BELOW: Mark Clark signs the Armistice agreement for the UN Command.

recognized the other's existence, and UNCURK was finally disbanded in 1977. The UN Command in Korea gradually withdrew, leaving only the Americans, who signed their treaty with South Korea in October 1953. Some UN members, like the British, still however supply observers to Panmunjon, where at irregular intervals the American representatives of the United Nations meet with the Chinese People's Volunteers and the Korean People's Army to discuss a Korean War that, technically, has never ended.

The United States has never been quite sure whether it won or lost the Korean War. Fighting for a draw, particularly a deliberate draw, is not something easy for Americans to grasp. Some still argue that 'We lost because we did not win,' others that in defeating communist aggression in Korea the United States laid the foundations for world peace. What is certain is that the war led to the massive rearmament of the United States, and to its assumption of the role of 'world policeman' in earnest in the next decade. The support given to America by the British Commonwealth in Korea, and the additional support given by France, Holland, Belgium and Turkey, helped cement the new NATO alliance. But the small size of all the European contingents, including the British, showed their diminished status in the new world order.

For the United Nations Korea was on the one hand a victory, which showed that the new organization had effective powers to stop war, and on the other a defeat, since the war convinced the Soviet Union that the UN was completely American dominated. Mao Tse-tung claimed the war as a victory. It had given him his breathing space to consolidate communist rule in China, and demonstrated that American atomic weapons were 'paper tigers.' But this had been achieved only with appalling losses, and at the cost of American hostility which kept China out of the UN until 1972. Conversely, Chiang Kai-shek in Taiwan retained power with American support, and without needing to fire a shot. The Japanese, also, benefitted greatly from the war. In cooperating with the Americans they earned their independence from occupation years before they might otherwise have done so.

In Korea itself, the North also claimed victory, but also at a fearful cost, not only in losses during the war but in the persistence of Kim Il Sung's government. To this day, he remains head of a country that is one of the poorest and least free in Asia. Syngman Rhee was probably saved from an internal revolt by the outbreak of the war. In the event, he lasted until a similar revolt overthrew him in 1960. South Korea prospered, and has become one of the richest of the Far East countries, although its rulers have seldom been democratic as the West uses the word. Perhaps the biggest loser was the Soviet Union. By failing to support North Korea more strongly Stalin lost much of his prestige in the Far East to the Chinese, but at the same time his actions convinced his former World War II allies in the West that the Soviet Union posed a massive and unpredictable military threat, and heightened the Cold War. In this sense, also, the Korean War has never ended.

BELOW: One of the many meetings of the Armistice Commission at Panmunjon held since the end of the Korean War.

Page numbers in *italics* refer to illustrations.

ACKNOWLEDGMENTS

The author and publishers would like to thank Ron Callow for designing this book, Mandy Little for the picture research and Pat Coward for the index. The following provided photographic material:
Bison Archive, pages: 2, 6, 12(below), 30(below), 31(both), 32(top), 33(below right), 43(below), 48(bottom 2), 49(below), 61, 66(top), 71(top), 75(top).
Chinese News Agency, pages: 9(below), 51(top left & below), 55(below), 63(top).
Hulton Picture Co, pages: 8(top), 9(top), 24, 25(top), 29(top), 33(below left), 38(center & below), 39(top & below right), 40(below), 43(top), 52, 60(top), 64(both), 69(top), 71.
Robert Hunt Library, pages: 8(below), 10(both), 11(both), 12(top), 13(top), 14, 15, 22(both), 25(below), 26(below), 27(both), 29(below), 34-35, 37(top), 38(top), 40(top), 41(both), 42, 46(top), 47(below), 57(all 3), 58-59, 62, 65, 68(top 2), 71(middle), 74(both), 76, 77(both), 78.
Imperial War Museum, London, pages: 32(below), 45(top), 56(top), 63(below right).
National Archives, pages: 26(top), 69(below).
Peter Newark's Western Americana, page: 16.
Warren Thompson. page: 70(top).
The Research House, pages: 18-19, 30(top), 33(top), 49(top), 66(middle), 67(below right).
The Research House/ Department of Defense, pages: 36, 39(left), 45(below).
The Research House/US Army, pages: 44(both), 75(below).
The Research House/US Navy, pages: 67(top & below left), 68(below).
Topham Picture Library, pages: 20, 47(top), 50(below), 53(top), 54(both), 56(below), 60(below), 70(below), 72(both).
US Army Photograph, pages: 1, 23, 28, 50(top), 53(below), 55(top), 63(below left), 73.
US Signal Corps Photograph, pages: 37(below), 51(top right), 66(below).
UPI/Bettmann Newsphotos, page: 46(below).